Practical Millinery Lessons • Julia Bottomley

*** *** *** *** *** *** *** ***

Practical Millinery Lessons

A COMPLFTE COURSE OF LESSONS IN THE

Art of Millinery

A Text Book for Teachers of Millinery;

A Guide (or the milliner in the workroom.

Especially planned to provide a complete course fur Home Study, for the novice.

Embraces all the difficult processes and methods which lighten the labor of the most experienced milliners.

Revised by

JULIA BOTTOMLEY

January. 1914

Published by

THE ILLUSTRATED MILLINER CO.

New York

Copyright 1914

by

The Illustrated Milliner Co.

New York

Entered According to Act of Congress In the Office of the Librarian of Congress, Washington, D. C.

PREFACE

The art of Millinery may be mastered by the purposeful and painstaking student who carefully perlorms each operation as taught herein. A course of printed lessons has certain advantages over other methods of acquiring a knowledge of the Art of Millinery. It is, of necessity, accurate; it is more explicit than the average course of oral instructions given in a class room; it is more systematic and covers a wider field than the training obtained by an apprentice in a millinery workroom, and in a printed course each lesson may be referred to whenever desired.

This course has been prepared with a threefold purpose:

First: To provide teachers with a text book complete, concise and thoroughly practical.

Second: It aims to aid the milliner in instructing her apprentice, for, if studied in a workroom and under the quidance of a milliner, the ideal conditions for learning the Art of Millinery are fulfilled.

Third: For Home Study, providing an ideal series of lessons for all who desire to master the art of millinery; and for those who have picked up some knowledge of millinery work and wish to perfect their methods.

PRACTICAL MILLINERY LESSONS

INDEX TO LESSONS

PREPARATION FOR LESSONS

The Work Table

Light — Necessary Tools— Findings

Necessary Materials

The Work Table.

A small table should be secured 36 inches long, 21 inches wide, and 26 inches high. These are the minimum dimensions. A longer and somewhat wider table of the same height serves as well. But it is desirable to learn to work with the amount of table surface given above. The table should be plain and substantial. A small kitchen table with legs shortened will answer every purpose.

This is to be covered with plain white oilcloth, tacked along the edges or the under side of the top, smoothly and neatly to the surface. When the top has been covered in this way, a plain tape measure may be tacked along one side at the edge; or with brass tacks indicate a yard, half yard, and the first nine inches. Such a table is easly kept clean. It should be fitted with one or two drawers on the under side and a rack at the back, on which boxes containing materials or finished work may be placed. A movable spool rack will be found a convenience; or two wire nails driven in at the right end will hold a spool of white and a spool of black millinery thread respectively, within handy reach. A plain, cane-seat chair and a small foot-rest will prove comfortable for the worker. The equipment of the table is finished by providing two substantial millinery hat boxes which are placed on the rack. One is for materials with which the student is working and the other for finished work. Have a square of cheese-cloth or muslin for covering work at night. Light.

Nothing is more essential than goo.d light. The light, should fall from above, and over the left shoulder of the worker, if possible. Sunlight should be diffused by a thin curtain or frosted glass. This makes the proper light for matching colors.

Necessary Tools and Findings.

The tools used by the beginner are few and simple. A well fitting thimble, a package of ordinary needles and one of millinery needles, two pairs of scissors, a pair of nippers (or pliers) for cutting and handling wire, a tape line, a very sharp knife or razor blade, a feather curling knife, a flat iron and holder. One pair of scissors should be tailor's shears with sharp points and about 8 inches long (including handles). A second short pair with blunt blade-ends will be found convenient for some purposes. Scissors made especially for cutting lace, net, chiffon, etc., are called "lace scissors" and are four or five inches long. One blade in these scissors is provided with a guard which prevents the scissors from catching in the mesh of the lace, or in any other soft fabric.

The worker should provide herself with white or light sewing aprons as a protection to her dress and to fabrics. A regular sewing apron with one or two ample pockets is easily laundered.

Crash is an excellent fabric for this purpose. Calico or nercale may be used.

NECESSARY MATERIALS.

The following materials are needed by the beginner; 1 piece white brace wire, either satin or mercerized. 1 piece black brace wire, either satin or mercerized. 1 spool white tie wire. 1 spool black tie wire. 1 spool uncovered tie wire. 1 spool millinery thread No. 24 (white). 1 spool millinery thread No. 24 (black). 1 spool Linen thread (No. 24 black.) 5 yards white millinery mull. 5 yards black millinery mull. 4 yards white buckram. 4 yard black buckram. 1 piece ribbon wire (white). 1 piece ribbon wire (black). 1 yard mercerized lining (black). 1 yard mercerized lining (white).

NECESSARY TOOLS. 1 package ordinary needles. 1 package millinery needles. Feather Curling Knife 1 paper millinery pins.

1 pair sharp pointed scissors, 8 inches long. 1 pair blunt end scissors. 1 pair lace scissors. 1 pair pliers (or nippers.) 1 tapeline. 1 knife. 1 feather curling knife. 1 flatiron and holder. LESSON I.

To Make a One-Piece Wire Frame.

The First Step.

The student should examine wire frames before attempting to do any work. Some frames are joined at the intersection of their wires by means of tie-wire and some are made without it. A mechanical device known as a frame machine is required for the latter variety known as the non-tie frame. Notice in hand made frames the method of binding the intersecting wires with tie wire which is twisted and clipped off short and the ends pressed down.

Use scraps of wire for practice.

Cutting wire with pliers.

Figure 1

The first thing to learn is to hold and cut wire with the pliers and the second, how to grasp and turn it with them. With the pliers cut up an old wire frame into bits 2 inches in length until you can cut the wire off squarely, so the covering will not unwrap. (See Figure 1.)

Practice turning the end of a bit of wire up by grasping it with the pliers and turning them in the hand. Next, practice fastening one piece over another firmly with tie-wire. (See Figure 2.) Hold the two bits of wire with first two fingers and thumb of the left hand and handle the tie-wire with pliers held in the right hand. Practice twisting the tiewire ends together around intersecting wires. (See Fig. 3.) Next cut them off within 1-4 inch of the intersection. Do not wrap tie wire about the brace wires more than once, else you will defeat your purpose, and instead of being firm, it will loosen and be bulky.

Wire frames are called one or two piece frames. Frames of the simplest outlines are made in one piece, while in other cases, the crowns and brims are made separately and set together afterward. Before proceeding to make a frame, the student must get in.mind the names and positions of those wires that outline the shape and determine its size. All the wires in a frame (except the tie-wire) are either "brace" or "stay" wires. The brace wires are those which extend from the crown to the edge of the brim and the stay wires are those which intersect them, extending in more or less circular outlines about the shape. One of these (that at the edge of the brim) is called the "edge-wire." Another (that which rests upon the head) is called the "headsize." (See Fig. 4.) In a one-piece frame the headsize and base of the crown are the same length. The wires at the top and base of the crown are called respectively the "top crown" and "base" wires. The wire is indicated in Figure 4. The student is to memorize the names and positions of the "edge-wire," "headsize," "top-crown," and "base" wires, for measurements of frames are taken by them.

Figure 4

Cut from a bolt of fine brace wire four pieces each 24 1-2 inches in length. Lay these four pieces together (like a bundle of sticks). At the center of the bundle, that is, midway between the ends, wrap a bit of tie-wire three times about

Figure 6 it and twist the ends of the tie-wire moderately tight, to hold the brace wires together. These wires are to form the

"brace" wires of the frame. Next, spread them apart as shown in Figure 5.

At a distance of 3 3-4 inches from the. center, where the wires have just been crossed, bend each wire downward at right angles to form the side of the crown. At the distance of 2 inches from the first bend, make another bend at right angles outward to form the brim.

Next step is to place a stay wire at the base of the crown; this is the headsize wire. It should be cut one inch longer than the circumference of the crown (to allow for lapping) and is therefore 24 3-4 inches long. Overlap the ends 1 inch and wind together with tie-wire. Slip this circle over the crown and tie it to all the brace wires. (See Fig. 4.) The overlapping ends of the headsize wire indicate the back of the frame.

The next step is to place the top crown wire, making a circle as for the headsize, placing the overlap at the back.

Measure off 60 inches of wire for the edgewire. This allows 1% inches for the overlap at the back. Next place the edge wire inside the upturned ends of the brace wire. These ends are bent back and pressed firmly over the edge wire. Tie-wire is wound about each intei section as already described, and the superfluous length cut away. (See Figure 4.)

Figure 6

Wire placed midway between crown wire and head-size.

Showing completion of frame.

The main wires of the frame are now in place and it is to be strengthened with 2 additional stay wires. These are placed midway between the top crown and headsize wires and midway between the brim edge and headsize wires. (See Fig. 6. The student is to measure the frame, the length required for these circles (allowing 1 inch for overlapping) and fasten them with tie-wire to the brace wires. This completes the frame.

LESSON II.

To Make a Two-piece Wire Frame.

It will be an easy matter for the pupil who has mastered Lesson I, to make the brim and crown illustrated in this lesson. According to instructions in Lesson

I, make the headsize A-B 18 1-2 inches in circumference. Make the edgewire C-D 34 inches in circumference. The stay wire circles are to be made by measuring the frame for the lengths

Cut off the brace wire (allowing 1 inch for turning over the headsize and edge wires) in the following lengts:

Front wire, (A-C) 4% inches, back wire (B-D) 5% in. Two side wires (M-N) 6 1-2 inches. Fasten the front brace wire over the headsize circle with tie-wire. Cut away any superfluous length of wire after fastening and press ends firmly down. Next adjust and fasten this wire to the edge wire circle. In the.same manner, fasten the back brace wire to place. Midway between the front and back brace wires, at each side, place the side brace wires. This outlines the frame.

Midway between the front and side brace wires, place an additional brace wire at each side. Also, midway between the back and side brace wires, place an additional brace wire making 8 brace wires in all.

The extra stay wire circles (E-F and G-H.) are finally slipped over the frame and tied to place completing the mushroom brim.

To Make a Round Crown.

The round crown is made as follows: Measure off 4 brace wires, each 19 inches long, one of which is designated in Figure 2 as C-F-J. Fasten these wires together at the center by wrapping tie-wire about them and spread them as in beginning a one piece wire frame. Turn the ends upward with the pliers to the depth of 1-2 inch.

Next make a top crown circle (A-B) (see Figure 2) from a piece of wire 14 inches long and a base crown circle (D-E) 21 inches long. Curve the brace wires downward and fasten the top crown and base wires to place. Midway between these wires place a third stay wire circle (I-J) and between this circle and the top crown and brace wires place stay wires (G-H) and (K-L). This completes the round crown. See Figure 2.

In hats made on two piece wire frames the brims and crowns are covered separately and afterwards sewed together.

The pupil should use a tape line to make all measurements. In placing additional stay wires in brim and crown, the tape line will serve to keep all intersections of brace and "staywires" equally distant from the headsize and thus preserve the symmetry of the frame.

A frame which is to be covered entirely with straw or silk braid may be made ready for use with uncovered tiewire. But a frame to be covered with lace or other transparent material, as maline, chiffon or lace braids, should be made with covered tie-wire.

A TWO-PIECE WIRE FRAME FOR A TURBAN

Nearly all turbans are made on two-piece frames similar to that shown in the illustration.

LESSON III.

The Stitches Used in Millinery.

In millinery, as in dress-making, different stitches are adapted to different parts of the work. There are, at least, ten important stitches which the student should practice making before taking up the making of hats. The name of each stitch must instantly picture to the mind of the sewer, the stitch itself. It is therefore necessary for the beginner to practice making these stitches and to memorize their names. They are as follows:

The Running Stitch, the Back Stitch, the Overcast Stitch, the Feather Stitch, the Buttonhole Stitch, the Under-hem Stitch, the Slip Stitch (also called the Blind Stitch),,the Stab Stitch, the Saddler's Stitch, the Lacing Stitch.

Stitches are designated as "short" or "long" without any definite basis of measurements. The student may consider that a stitch over one-eighth of an inch in length is long. The terms apply properly with reference to stitches used for sewing. Basting stitches are much longer.

rig. 1 The Fly-running Stitcb. Fig. 2 Back Stitch.

Fig. 1. The Fly-running Stitch is used for shirring and gathering fabrics. The needle is run through the fabric from one side to the other and back, in stitches of 'even length. The material is crowded on the needle until half its length is filled. The thread (which has been knotted) is drawn through and the operation repeated.

When the fabric is not crowded on the needle nor afterward fulled on the thread, the stitch is used for seams, hems and many other parts of the work. It is also called the plain running stitch.

Fig. 2. The Back-stitch is used to sew two thicknesses of material together firmly. In sewing bias strips of velvet together along the selvedge or in joining firmly any fabrics, this stitch is employed. The needle takes up a single stitch in the fabric. It is then pulled through. For the next stitch the needle is thrust through the fabric half-way back toward the beginning of the first stitch,and each succeeding stitch back upon the last stitch made.

Fig. 3. The Over-cast ititch is frequently ued. As its name implies, the stitch is made by throwing or casting the thread over an edge or edges placed together. Edges of folds are joined by the Over-cast stitch.

Two edges sewed together by a shallow over-cast stitch, are said to be "whipped" together. Nothing is taken away from the width of materials in this way.

When it is desirable to gather laces or other fabrics along the extreme edge, an overcast-stitch is run along over the edge and the fabric fulled or gathered in this manner instead of by the fly running stitch. In Fig. 3 the portion marked "B" shows the over-cast stitch used for joining edges and the portion marked "A" indicates the stitch as used for gathering fabrics. Wire is often applied to edge of buckram by this stitch.

Fig. 4 The feather stitch is illustrated here. Single short running stitches are used to make the feather stitch. The needle is thrust, for the second stitch, below and ahead of the first stitch and pointing toward it. It is then pulled through and the next stitch taken a little ahead and on a line with the first stitch. *By* continuing to sew in this *way,* two parallel rows of the plain running stitch appear on one side of the fabric, joined *by* diagonal threads on the side toward the sewer. The feather stitch is used in sewing ribbon wire to ribbon, in laying flat seams open and in other ways. It is an ornamental stitch when made evenly and is used in fancy work.

Fig. 6 Buttonhole Stitch. Fig. 6 Under Hem Stitch.

Fig. 5. The buttonhole stitch is used for sewing wire on edges, in finishing work, to hold other stitches, so as to fasten the thread securely, and for applique work. It is an over-cast stitch in which the thread is thrown around the needle when it is thrust through from the under to the upper side of the fabric. When the stitches are set close together a firm edge is produced, such as is required in buttonholes. This stitch is employed in making them.

Fig. 6. The under hem stitch is used for flat hemming. The needle is thrust through a bit of the fabric and a short simple running stitch taken up. It is then thrust through the raw edge from the under side and pulled through.

Fig. 7. No Stitch is more useful in millinery than the slip or blind stitch. It is used in hemming veils and other fabrics, sewing in facings, making rolled edges, drawing together turned in edges o(velvet, and in high-class millinery is much employed. The needle takes up a simple running stitch in the fabric and is thrust through the turned under edge immediately above this running stitch, and pulled through. By taking up a tiny shred of the fabric each time a new stitch is made, the sewing is made invisible on both sides of the fabric. The name "slip-stitch" comes from the fact that the needle is slipped through the turned edge.

Fig. 8' The Stab stitch is a simple stitch employed when sewing a heavy fabric, such as buckram, and when applying trimming to a hat. The needle is thrust through the fabric and the thread pulled through. It is then thrust back from the other side.

Fig. 9. The saddler's stitcn is a stitch used for flat folds and seams. This stitch is taken under each raw edge and they are drawn together.

Fig. 10. The lacing stitch is used when making a round fold or for drawing two edges together. A simple running stitch is placed first in one edge and then in the opposite edge, as shown in the picture. By drawing the thread firmly the edges are turned inside the fold. If it is simply desired to bring the edges together the thread is not tightly drawn, but is left in the position shown in the picture.

LESSON IV.

To Cover a Wire Frame With Mull.

Wire frames must be first covered with mull or some other suitable fabric to provide a foundation before they are covered with braid.

The material must set smoothly to the frame without drawing it out of shape. (See Figure 1.)

Take the frame made in Lesson 1, lay it on a piece of mull and outline the edge wire with chalk or pencil. Allowing 1-2 inch about the edge to turn over the edge wire of the frame. Cut the outlined circle from the mull. Using this as a guide, cut a second circle like it, for the underbrim covering.

Prom the center of one circle cut out a small circle with a diameter 1 inch shorter than the diameter of the headsize. Slash the mull to the depth of half an inch all around the small circular opening, (See Figure 2). Slip the mull prepared in this way over the crown of the wire frame and pin the edge at intervals over the edge wire and about the headsize. Sew it about the headsize first, holding it smooth. Without stretching the mull or the frame out of shape, sew the edge of the mull over the edge wire of the frame. This completes the upper brim covering.

The headsize is not to be cut from the underbrim covering until after it is sewed to place over the edgewire. Pin the underbrim covering smoothly to place and sew it over the edgewire. Next cut a small circle at the center, allowing 1-2 inch to turn up into the crown. Slash the circle to the depth of 1-2 inch, turn the slashes into the crown and sew to the headsize wire. This covers the under brim.

Cut a circular piece of mull for the top crown, allowing a half inch about the edge to turn down over the side crown, and pin it to the frame. Cut out tiny gores to get rid of the extra fulness about the side crown, and sew the mull to the brace wires overlapping the edge of the gores.

For the side crown cut a strip of mull, on the bias, one inch wider than the height of the crown, and one inch longer than the distance around the base. Turn each edge and one end of this strip under to the depth of one-half inch and lay it about the side crown, overlapping the ends at the back. Place the turned-under end over the other end and sew together. Tack this crown covering to the brace wires and to the brim and crown coverings. This completes the covering of a plain sailor shape as shown in Figure 1.

How to Cover a Round Crown With Mull.

Measure across the crown, Figure 3, along one brace wire, from the base of the crown at one side to the opposite point at the base, and take this length plus one inch as the diameter of a circular piece of mull to be cut for covering the crown. Cut the circle from the mull and place its center over the center of the top crown at "C" (Figure 3). Tack the mull to the frame here. Figure 4 shows the plaque of mull tacked to the frame with gores indicated which may be necessary to cut out or to lay in small side plaits.

Smooth the mull over the crown and pin the edges at the middle front, back and sides over the wire at the base of the crown. Midway between these points, smooth and pin the mull over the base wire. The extra fulness of mull may be disposed of by laying it in plaits, by slashing the mull and overlapping the slashed edge or by cutting out small gores. The first method is the one generally used.

In using the side plait for disposing of fulness, several small plaits will cover the frame more neatly than fewer large plaits. When gores are cut out the mull is smoothed over the frame and slashed up to the beginning of extra fulness, after pinning to the base as just directed. The overlapping edges are cut away allowing about one-half inch overlap to remain. This is tacked, with long easy stitches, to the underlying mull. When the extra fulness is not cut out in a gore, the overlapping edge is smoothed over the underlying mull and held in place by the turn over the base of the crown. This or the method of plaiting are to be used when frames are covered with straw braids or other fabrics that are opaque. When the covering is of thin lace, lacy braids or other transparent fabrics, and the mull covering must be made as inconspicuous as possible, it is best to cut out gores in fitting the mull.

With practice the student will learn to dispose of much extra fulness by the simple method of stretching the mull in the direction opposite to that of the fulness. For instance, the mull covering in Figure 4 may be gently stretched in the directions "C-A" and "C-B," "C-L," and at all other portions of its circumference. But care must be taken not to pull the wire frame out of shape. Very neat work is done in covering by this method of stretching. Some fulness will"still remain to be disposed of as directed above.

To Cover a Rolling Brim.

Measure across the brim from side to side (at its widest part) and use this measurement for the diameter of the plaque of mull for the brim covering by increasing it one inch. Cut from the center of this large plaque a small circle one inch less in diameter than the headsize. This circular opening in the mull plaque is to be evenly stretched to fit the headsize of the brim (indicated by "A-B-C-D" in Figure 5.)

The mull plaque is to be stretched and smoothed over the brim, pinned over the edgewire at the middle of the front, back and sides as indicated in Figure 5 by "E-F-G-H" and midway between these points. After smoothing and stretching the mull over the brim, the superfluous fulness is to be disposed of at the brim edge by any of the three methods given for the crown. The edge of the plaque is to overlap the edgewire of the frame and is to be sewed to place. Any extra width of mull resulting from the stretching process must be trimmed away about the edge.

Where brims are fluted or flare much, it is necessary to insert a gore of mull in the plaque wherever needed. In this case the plaque is to be slashed and gores cut, sufficiently large to overlap the edge of the slashes.

LESSON V.

To Sew Braid to a Wire Frame.

When the student can make a wire frame and can cover it with mull so that it is shapely and neat looking, she is ready for the next step in hat-making. This is the sewing of braids to the covered frame. This lesson sets forth the best and most popular of the various methods of covering the frame with straw braid. There are almost inumerable fanciful ways of sewing braids but the learner must first master the simple methods.

Braids as a rule are light in weight, very pliable, and of a convenient width. *As* recently manufactured, they are not difficult to sew. If a braid is stiff or brittle, and breaks when one attempts to sew it, it must be moistened before it can be sewed to the frame. It may be placed in a zinc lined box over night and covered with a cloth which has been dipped in water and wrung, leaving it damp, or held over a steaming kettle of water wrapped in a damp cloth and allowed to remain until pliable.

For covering the frame select a pliable braid a little more than an inch in width. For the beginner it is best to choose a rather loosely woven braid having a narrow fancy finish at one edge. Sew with a short thread to prevent it from snarling and pull stitches moderately tight. When a silkstraw is to be used, select a silk thread matching it in color, to sew with. If a dull finish braid is selected, choose a mercerized cotton thread. In other words, choose a thread matching the braid in surface finish as well as in color.

This thread should be smooth, firm and moderately heavy. No. 30 to No. 50 will usually be found the best selection. A strong, short needle should be used, as fine as will carry the thread easily.

Sew the braid in parallel rows to the frame, with one edge of each row overlapping very slightly the row preceding it. This method is called the "row on row" method.

Beginning at the middle of the edge-wire at the back of the frame, fold the ends of the braid over the edge using it as a binding. Sew it to place, from right to left, using the stab stitch about one-fourth inch in length. Hold the braid smoothly to the shape, stretching slightly if necessary. When this braid binding has been sewed entirely around the brimedge, allow one and one-half inches of braid at the end to lap over the beginning of the binding. Cut the braid from the bolt at this point; slope the braid to the under brim and tack to place with several stitches. This completes binding the frame with the braid.

Sometimes the edge is bound with velvet or silk, cut in bias strips, instead of braid. It is placed in the manner just described.

Beginning at the back again, holding the end of the braid in the left hand (the bolt lying in the lap) a row of braid is sewed to the upper brim with its outer edge even with the bound edge of the frame. Hold the braid smoothly at the shape, stretching it slightly at the outer edge and sewing it at the inner edge. Thrust the needle through from upper to under brim and back as in sewing the binding. When this first row has been sewed to place until it entirely encircles the brim edge, the braid is not cut at the back.

It is gradually sloped in toward the base of the crown, until it becomes a second row overlapping the first, oneeighth of an inch or a little more. Very wide braids have to be cut and pointed at the back, but narrow braids are continued round and" round the brim until the base of the crown is reached. See Figure 2.

Most brims are wider at the front than at the back or if not at that point, they widen at other points, so that an equal number of rows of braid will not cover the brim at all positions.

In this case short lengths of braid have to be used to complete the covering. These terminate at the base of the crown with about one-half inch allowed at each end, to extend up to the side crown where these ends are sewed down very firmly to place.

Covering the Top Crown.

The covering for the top crown is to be made next. This is made separately as a rule and sewed to the top crown afterward. To make it, wind the end of the piece of braid with thread to prevent raveling and turn it under one-half inch to conceal it. Tack it down with a few stitches. Holding the end thus prepared in the right hand, fold the braid in plaits to form a small circle. The plaits are laid in the plain edge of the braid. If the braid is loosely woven, it can be gathered along the straight edge to form the small circle. After forming the center, as shown in Figure 1, do not cut the braid but slope it out and sew it under the edge of the circle. Conceal the stitches as much as possible by making them very short on the upper side of the plateau you are making.

Make this plateau one-half inch greater in diameter than the top of the frame and allow one and one-half inches of braid to slope under at the end. Tack this to place and thus complete the top crown.

Sew this plateau to the top crown of the covered frame, placing the center of the braid plateau above the center of the crown. Sew along the edge of the top crown of the frame, concealing the stitches. The edge of this plateau will extend one-quarter inch beyond the edge of the top crown.

Covering The Side Crown.

The side crown may be covered with the braid, having the fancy edge upstanding, or the reverse. Beginning at the back or at a point on the side crown near the top where the trimming is to be placed, sew down the end of the braid after previously winding it with thread to keep it from raveling. Place the fancy edge against the edge of the top crown and stretch slightly against the side crown. Sew along the straight edge. When the first row extends entirely around the crown near the top, do not cut the braid but gradually slope it downward until the fancy edge overlaps the plain edge oneeighth inch. Sew the second row of braid around the crown; continue to sew around until the side crown is covered. At the end turn an inch up into the inside crown and tack it there.

Second Method.

When the fancy edge is turned down instead of up the first row is placed at the base of the crown instead of the top edge and at the latter point the last row is stretched flat to the hat and does not meet the protruding edge of the crown. This edge extends out over the side crowns. When the side crown is completely covered, the braid is cut squarely off and turned under where it is tacked firmly down to the frame. This completes the simple and always popular "row on row" method of sewing the braid to the frame.

To Sew Lace Braids.

Lace braids are usually manufactured with a gathering thread along their straight edge. Before sewing them to the frame they are fulled into a ruffle. The fullness must be disposed evenly and may be arranged in flutings by tacking the braid at regular intervals to the shape.

Lace braids are also laid in side or box plaits and sewed to the frame row on row. Such braids are frequently sewed into circles, squares, hexagons and fanciful forms, and these forms afterward sewed to the shape, completely or partially covering it. Two kinds of braids are sometimes used on the same frame. Lace braids are often sewed across the frame from side to side. They are crowded on the top crown, with the rows diverging gradually as they approach the brim edge. When this method is used the braid is sewed to the under brim as well as to the upper brim and terminates in the headsize.

LESSON VI.

Wiring and Lining a Straw Hat.

Some pressed shapes and certain other hats have to be wired to support them. For this purpose ordinary brace wire is used, if it is to be concealed by a facing or other covering. If it is not to be covered, satin wire matching the shape in color is used.

Correct Stitches

The buttonhole stitch is used in applying wire to a brim if the wire is to be afterwoods covered. (See Fig. 1). The needle is thrust under the wire and through a fibre of the braid, catching a bit of the covering of the wire at the same time. It is thrust diagonally under the braid, and the thread is thrown under the point for each stitch. This fastens the wire firmly to the shape.

A silk covered wire, which is not to be concealed by a covering is carefully sewed to conceal the stitches. This is done by bringing the needle through a little fibre of the straw and taking a small bit of the covering of the wire on the needle from the underside. (See Pig. 2). The thread is then pulled through. Thrust the needle back at an angle from right to left through the straw again, and then proceed to make the second stitch. In this way the stitches are all under the wire and are not visible. A fine needle and silk thread matching the braid in colors should be *used.*

To Place The Wire.

Having selected the wire to be used, measure off a length sufficient to encircle the brim of the hat within an inch or more of the edge, allowing an inch for overlapping.

When joining the ends of wire, unwind the silk covering from each end a half inch and cut off one-quarter inch of the wire. Lap the ends over and take the silk threads, which were unwound and wind them back over the overlapping ends.

Lining the Hat.

Crown linings usually consist of two parts, a crown tip and a side crown lining. They are made of various fabrics, such as thin silks, mull, chiffon, cambric or net and lining materials.

To Cut the Lining.

Measure the length about the headsize and allow an extra inch for the length of the lining. The height of the crown from center to headsize determines the width of the lining.

The lining may be cut either crosswise, lengthwise, or bias of the goods. After cutting it the proper length, turn down the edge along one side to the depth of one-half inch for a hem and sew in the hem by hand or machine stitching. A tiny ribbon is to be run in the hem.

Before sewing in this lining, tack a small piece of it against the top of the inside crown, without allowing the stitches to show on the top crown. This tip usually carries the name of the establishment that made the hat. Either the overcast stitch or the buttonhole stitch is used for sewing in the lining as shown in Figure 4.

To Place the Lining.

Fold one end of the lining back one-half inch. Place this end at the middle of the back of the crown with the raw edge in the crown. Sew te linine to the headsize, allowing onehalf inch to extend into the crown. Sew from right to left, and continue until the lining is placed. At the back the turned-under end will lie over the other end. Sew firmly to nlace and sew the two ends together as far as the hem with plain running stitches.

The baby ribbon is run in the hem with a bodkin. It should be caught firmly with a few stitches at the half way point of the hem. Slip the bodkin (thread it with the ribbon) in the hem of the lapped-over seam at the back and when coming to the same point, thrust the bodkin right through the lining. This brings the ends of the ribbon on top to tie in a pretty bow.

LESSON VII.

How to Make and Use Bandeaux.

Many hats require a bandeau. It is obvious that the same shape will not fit all heads because of variations in the size and contour and in styles of hairdressing.

The purposes of a bandeau:-to reduce the headsize or to increase the headsize, or to make possible a definite poise of the hat on the head. To accomplish these there are

Fig. 1 Bandeau with Wire Whipped on Edge.

three staple shapes of bandeaux. They are a "straight" bandeau, the "flaring" bandeau, and the "halo" or round bandeau used in posing large crowned hats to the head:roperly.

Materials Used.

Bandeaux are foundations cut from buckram or rice net, bound with wire, and covered with velvet or other fabric. Having learned to make one correctly the pupil may, by using a pattern, make all the others correctly.

To Make a Bandeau.

Cut from buckram a bandeau like that shown in the picture (Fig. 1). Beginning in the middle of the top, sew a piece of brace wire, with an overcast stitch about the edge, as shown in Fig. 1. Keep the wire on the surface of the

Fig.'! Drjiw tin' Kdges of tlie Velvet with:i Long Stitcli.

buckram even with the edge. Allow the ends to overlap about one inch bringing one below the other. Use a strong, short needle and millinery thread.

To Cover a Bandeau.

Cut a strip of velvet on the bias M' inch longer than the bandeau at its widest part. Baste this to the buckram foundation with a long stitch and cut the shape of the bandeau, allowing Vi inch all around for overlapping the edge.

Next draw the edges of the velvet over the buckram foundation, as shown in Fig. 2, so that it will cover one side of the buckram foundation smoothly. Then cut and pull out the bastings.

If the bandeau is to be lined with same material with which it is covered, it makes no difference which side is covered first. But if the lining is of another fabric, it is well to place the outside covering first. The outside is the side to which the wire is sewed. This should not rest against the head, because it is liable to wear out quickly and to be uncomfortable.

b'K. 'i Iliiiuleiu Covered with Ilias Strip.

To Line the Bandeau.

From a bias strip of silk or velvet, cut the lining, allowing i/ inch to turn in all around. Baste this to the inside of the bandeau. Turn in the edge of the lining even with the bandeau, and sew to place with a short slip stitch. Use silk thread to match the covering.

When the bandeau is quite regular in shape it may be covered with a bias strip % inch wider than twice the width of the bandeau at its widest part. This is folded over the fondation, trimmed along the top edge and sewed, as shown in Fig 3. Both edges of the velvet are brought to the outside of the foundation. This pro-vides a smooth surface to rest against the head.

In covering an irregular bandeau it is often necessary to flash the edges of the covering to make it fit. (See Fig. 2). At the other points it may be necessary to cut or clip out little gores of the covering in order to avoid making a bulky finish.

Bandeau With Extension.

A bandeau is sometimes cut with an extension as shown in Fig. 4. The extension is not covered, but is thrust into the hat, where it forms a support for the trimming which is to be sewed on. For hats of lace braid, tulle, or lace, such an arrangement is often necessary. The bandeau portion is covered with a fabric, as usual. The piece extending into the crown may be straight, curved or pointed at the top, ac cording to the shape of the crown in which it is used. The "halo" is neatly covered by cutting out a circle of velvet or other fabric $y2$ inch greater in diameter than the foundation. This is basted to the buckram and the headsize cut out, allowing J/j inch all around to overlap the edge of the foundation. The edges of velvet are flashed and drawn together, and a lining finally placed as in other bandeaux. It is not absolutely essential to line the halo. The outside covering may be machine stiched to the foundation about i/g inch from the edges, as the inner surface is not visible.

LESSON VIII.

Drafting Patterns For Buckram Frames and Taking Paper Patterns From Buckram Shapes.

Before attempting to copy frames one must learn to draft a pattern. A short-back sailor with a plain crown should be first undertaken, as the steps necessary for this simple rig. i

First steps in cutting a circle from a square.

shape will familiarize the student with the general principles of pattern making. One next learns to change and vary this shape. This knowledge applied to more intricate methods enables the learner to draft patterns of all the shapes that it is possible to copy.

How to Cut a Plain Brim.

Take a square of manila paper eighteen inches across as shown in Fig. 1. The sides of the square are designated by the lines "A-B", "A-C", "B-D" and "C-D". Bisect each side of the square. The points of bisection are designated by the letters "E", "F", "G" and "H." Draw a line from E to F and one from G to H. These lines will intersect at the point marked "I" in the diagram. This is the center of rig. 2

Folding for tUe Circle.

the square. Fold the square of paper along the line "G-H" and fold the oblong thus obtained along the line "E-I." The result is a square one-tourth as large as the original. Fold this small square along the diagonal "B-I." The result is a triangle as shown in Fig. 2. By folding this triangle so that the side "A-C" lies along the other side from "A" to "B" and cutting from "C" to "B" in a slight curve, a fairly accurate circle results. Repeated foldings make the circle more nearly perfect.

A Second Method

A second method is simply to find the center of the square of manila paper as already described, and to make this the center of a circle drawn within the square. This is easily done by tying a piece of string about a pin pushed into the center of the square. This piece of string is one-half as long as a side of the square and becomes the radius of the circle drawn by means of it. Draw the circle and cut it out from the square. This circular piece of paper becomes the brim pattern when the small circle for the headsize is cut out. In Fig. 3. the method of finding the position of the headsize is shown by the diagram. The circular piece of paper is folded so that the point on its circumference marked "C" is 3 inches in, from the point marked "B." C and B indicate the ends of a diameter of the circle. The resulting line "A-E" does not pass through the center of the large circle but its middle point "D" becomes the center of a small circle having a radius of 3 inches. Its circumference be comes the crown line or headsize of the pattern as designated in Fig. 3. After cutting the small circle from the larger one we have a pattern as shown in Fig. 4.

The small circular piece cut out should be kept to use as a pattern of the headsize in drafting other brim patterns. It is obvious to the pupil that by placing this pattern on the larger circle near the front brim-edge. A narrow front and a wide back brim results. If it is desired that the left brim be wider than the right, the headsize pattern is placed nearer the right brim-edge and vice versa. The width of the brim at any point depends upon the position of the headsize.

The Crown.

The simplest of crown patterns for this brim will consist of a top crown cut by the headsize pattern and a straight strip one inch longer than the length of the circumference of the

Fig. 5 Large Circle Cut for Side-crown Pattern.

crown. This strip is varied in width according to the height of the crown desired. A strip 22 inches long and 3 inches wide will form a side crown pattern for a "straight Crown," allowing sufficient length for overlapping.

Sloping Crowns.

Many shapes have crowns sloping outward from the base to the top. Such crowns are called "bell" crowns. The reverse of this, that is, a crown larger at the base than at the top is called a sloping crown. To draft a side crown pattern for a sloping crown or a bell crown one must first cut a very large semi-circle from paper. This semi-circle should have a radius equal in length to the diameter of the circle cut for the brim, or larger. Having drawn the semi-circle with radius of 18 inches designated by the letters A-D-B in Fig. 5. one may take a side crown pattern from it. Measure the height of the crown desired, say 3 inches on the radius (marked "D-C" in the diagram). Draw a second semi-circle having the same center ("C") as the first and a radius of 15 inches. Cut away the second semi-circle. The resulting circular strip, 3 inches wide, will serve as a pattern of a side crown. The crown will slope more or less as the circle is large or small. The length of the strip equals the circumference of the crown.

Fancy Brim.

When one wishes to vary the flat brim and cause it either to flare or droop or' roll it is necessary to slash it in order to give it a greater or a less length of edge. By cutting out a "V" shaped piece and bringing the edges together or overlapping them, the brim is drawn downward. By slashing the brim and inserting a "V" shaped gore the brim is made to flare or undulate, or allowed to roll. The pupil will gather from the diagrams in Figs. 6, 7 and 8, how plain brims are varied and pattern drafted for fancy ones.

Almost all shapes used are bought ready for covering. Nevertheless a milliner is expected to know how to make a buckram shape. She may find herself called upon to copy a shape, to modify one, or to design one. It is therefore, necessary to understand how to proceed to convert a piece of buckram into a hat shape.

There are some shapes that cannot be exactly copied unless the milliner has "dies" or forms over which to mold the buckram. This is especially true of crowns. These peculiar crowns are made to sell separately by the manufacturer, and are a great assistance to the milliner in developing new ideas from a single shape.

Taking Paper Patterns From Hats. To copy a frame by taking a pattern from it, one requires a quantity of tissue paper, some pins and paste, a lead pencil and a pair of small, sharp scissors.

To Pin Paper to the Shape

Take the shape to be copied and pin the edge of a piece of paper to the edge of the brim at the widest portion of the brim and pin it down at intervals as long as the conformation of the brim allows the paper to lie smoothly. Cut the paper along the lines of the brim edge and headside. If the brim is very irregular the pattern must be taken in sections and afterward pasted together. By smoothing paper over portions of the brim and cutting the pattern in as many sections as are necessary to reproduce the brim's irregularities, the brim may be exactly copied. Mark the middle of the front, back and sides with a lead pencil mark.

The Side Crown Pattern

The side crown pattern is taken by pinning one edge of the paper to the side crown at the top edge, smoothing the paper and pinning it at the base of the crown. It may be necessary to cut this portion of the pattern in sections. The middle of the front, back and sides must be marked with a pencil so that the frame cut from this pattern can be put together accurately. The top crown pattern is taken in the same way.

If the pattern cut is to be kept it should be pasted to a crinoline foundation. As patterns conform exactly to the shapes from which they are cut, no allowance is made for joinings and turnings in the buckram. This allowance is made at the time the frame is cut from the buckram. When cutting a crinoline foundation these allowances may be made in it. The are as follows: One-half inch on inside of crown line or headsize. One-half inch at each end of side crown. After these allowances are made in the crinoline or pattern, the buckram is to be cut exactly like it.

Almost all shapes used are bought ready for covering. Nevertheless a milliner is expected to know how to make a buckram shape. She may find herself called upon to copy a shape, to modify one, or to design one. It is, therefore, necessary to understand how to proceed to convert a piece of buckram into a hat shape.

There are some shapes that cannot be exactly copied unless the milliner has "dies" or forms over which to mold the buckram. This is especially true of crowns. These peculiar crowns are made to sell separately bv the manufacturer, and are a great assistance to the milliner in developing new ideas from a single shape.

LESSON IX.

How to Make Buckram Frames

The student is to cut and put together a hat frame cut by pattern shown in Figure 1. The same processes apply in all frames, plain or fancy, except for the latter, some additional steps are taken as will be shown in this lesson.

Fig. 1

To Cut the Frame.

In Fig. 1, the pattern is shown laid out on a length of buckram from which it is to be cut. In order to be economical the pattern should be laid on the buckram with the middle of the front brim on a bias line across one corner and the remaining pieces as close to this circle as possible. Outline the pattern on the buckram with a pencil and cut it out, allowing % inch inside the headsize to slash and turn up into a crown.

In cutting the side crown allow 1 inch to the end for overlapping. Having cut the buckram, slash the headsize at intervals % inch to the depth of % inch all around. The student will proceed to stay the several parts with wire.

Fig. 2 Sewing on Brace Wire. Fig. g Sewing the Side Crown to Brim.

Use a brace wire such as is used in making frames and overcast it about the brim edge. Hold the wire even with the brim edge on top of the frame and begin at the middle of the back brim to sew it to the buckram. Use the short overcast stitch and do not allow the wire to slip off the edge of the brim. Overlap the ends at the back and fasten finally with button hole stitches sewed in firmly and close together.

To Brace the Frame.

After the brim edge is wired, the brim is to be braced with ribbon wire to prevent it from dropping from the crown and to aid in giving it an upward or downward turn if desired.. In Figure 2, brace wires are seen placed to the frame. Place one at the middle of the front, one at the middle of the back and one at each side. Midway between these place other wires, making eight in all. These are to be cut the exact length required to reach from the edgewire to the inner edge of the headsize opening, that is, the width of the brim, including slashes, in each case, and feather-stitched to place with millinery thread. After placing these wires, turn up the half inch allowance which has been slashed, and the brim is finished.

In sewing ribbon wire to place, thrust the needle through the tape and buckram just inside the tiny outer wire. Wiring the Side Crown.

Wire the upper and lower edge of the side crown with brace or shirring wire in the same manner as the brim. Overlap the ends of side crown 1 inch and feather stitch them together. This completes the side crown.

To Sew the Parts Together.

Slip the crown over the slashes about the headsize, placing the overlapped portion at the side or wherever the trimming is to be placed. The slashes thus extend up into the crown. Sew the side crown and brim firmly together using a back stitch and strong millinery thread. Draw the thread firmly in each stitch. In Figure 3 the side crown is about to be tacked at its base to the brim. It should be tacked at the front, back and sides, after which it is overcast to the top of the side crown all around. This completes the frame.

Sometimes the top crown is sewed in without wiring and in other cases the top crown is wired and the top of the side crown left unwired. The side crown may be cut % inch wider than the pattern, slashed to this depth and turned under the wired top crown. These are simply variations in the matter of placing the top crown piece and any one of them is correct.

In order that the wires may not show through the fabric with which the frame is to be covered, the brim is to be bound with narrow strips of crinoline. Cut the strips % inch wide and sew them smoothly about the brim edge and top crown edge. That about the top crown will be placed with one edge on the top crown and one on the side crown. Stretch the fabric to make it lie smoothly to place. In order to stretch it, it must be cut on the true bias.

To Make a Mushroom Brim.

A mushroom brim is made by using the segment of a very large circle cut from buckram instead of a flat piece for the brim. Cut a semi-circle having a diameter 4 times as long as the diameter of the brim required. Measure off on the circumference of this large circle the length of brim edge required plus 1 inch for overlapping and mark the point with

Flg. 4 Dome Crown in Process of Making.

pencil. At this point cut from the circle a segment, making the piece as wide as the brim at its widest part. Allow % inch along the shorter edge for slashing and turning into the headsize.

Slash the edge of this brim at intervals with $y2$ or 2 inches to half its depth all around and overlap the slashed edges to produce the downward curve of the brim. Feather stitch the overlapping edges together and wire the brim edge.

To Make a Dome or Round Crown.

Cut from buckram a circle having a diameter equal to the length of the crown de.=ired fvom side to side across the top. Slash the circle at intervals of $y2$ or 2 inches about the edge to within 3 inches of the top for the average round crown. Overlap the slashed edges and pin them together, increasing or decreasing the overlap until the required curve is produced. In Fig. 5 a round crown is shown in process of making.

After the crown has been properly shaped by overlapping the slashed edges, and the overlappings feather stitched together, wire the lower edge with brace wire and strengthen the crown with wire braces if necessary.

When the student has mastered the foregoing process she will be able to undertake to copy or alter buckram frames of any description.

Rice net and willow foundations are used as well as buckram and are manipulated in about the same manner. Where a light frame, not rigid, is required, rice net is often employed. When lightness and much durability are desired, willow foundations are used or featherweight buckram.

LESSON X.

To Cover Buckram Frames With Velvet.

Select a plain buckram frame, such as is shown in Figure 1, to cover with velvet. The frame has a flat brim and what is known as a "square," sloping crown. Having learned to

Fig. 1

Plain Buckram

Frame.

cover such a frame the beginner is prepared to cover others of more irregular outline with velvet or other fabrics.

Patterns Necessary.

Having selected the frame, the student must cut a pattern of it from paper. This pattern is to be used in cutting out the velvet covering and the interlining.

To Cut the Pattern.

Place a strip of tissue paper, three times as long as the measurement of the brim from the center front to the centre back, on a table. Place the frame on the paper with the underbrim downward, and'draw with a lead pencil, the the outline of the brim. Mark the middle of the front and middle of the back brim with an "X" and cut out, with sharp scissors, the circular piece thus drawn, following the outline exactly. Mark this piece "facing." Using.this pattern as a guide cut another exactly like it from tissue paper, nicking the middle of the back and front with an X.

To cut the Headsize.

Next pin the tissue paper pattern to the under brim so that the pattern coincides with the frame. As the tissue paper is semi-transparent one can see the outline of the head size. This is to be drawn lightly with a leadpencil and cut out. Mark the center front and center back as before and write the words "upper brim" on this pattern.

An outline of the top crown is next to be drawn on the paper. Place the top crown downward on the manila and draw its outline, marking the middle of the front and back with an "X." Cut along the marking for pattern of the top crown. Write "top crown" on this piece.

The Side Crown Pattern.

Smooth a strip of tissue paper about the side crown, pinning it down to the frame. Draw with lead pencil the outline of the upper and lower edges of the side crown, and cut the pattern marking the middle of the front with an "X." Having cut the entire pattern according to these directions, write "front" and "back" at these points as designated by the markings.

Sometimes the side crown has no slope. In this jase a straight strip, as wide as the crown is high, and as long as the circumference of the crown, forms the pattern of the side crown.

To Cut the Velvet Covering.

Velvet must be cut so that the "pile" lays one way, in order that it may appear uniform in shade on the hat. It is very necessary therefore to place the pattern correctly, otherwise the hat may look as if made of two kinds of /elvet.

Lay a strip of velvet on the worktable with the pile side down. Lay the pattern on the velvet as shown in Figure 2. You will notice that the middle of the front of each piece is laid out on a bias line of the fabric, and that these fronts are all turned the same direction. It is essential that the pattern be placed in this way. Besides making the pile all lay in one direction, it makes easier the perfect fitting of the velvet to the frame.

Having placed the pattern on the velvet draw its outline with tailors' chalk and proceed to cut the velvet. Allow V4 inch margin around the outer edges and headsize of the brim coverings, % inch is to be allowed on each edge of the side crown and about the top crown, and % inch extra length for overlapping at the ends of the side crown. Nick the fronts and backs as marked on the patterns. Next, cut from fabric, (mull, hat lining or other thin fabric) an interlining for the hat, precisely like the covering just cut out.

To Place The Interlining

Pin the facing to the underbrim, at the brim edge so that the middle of the front coincides with that of the brim. Next pin the back and the sides. Do not stretch the fabric, but smooth it easily to the shape, pinning it at intervals all around the brim edge. Next, turn the edge up over the edgewire of the frr. me and baste down. Cut away any extra fulness about the edge by slashing out small "V" shaped piecesCut out t'.ie headsize allowing Vz inch to turn up into the crown. Sk.sh this edge at intervals of y inch all around and turn the flashes up into the crown, sewing the interlining to place here.

Slash the headsize of the upper brim covering, in the same way, to the depth of a scant i/ inch, and slip the covering over the crown of the hat. Proceed to adjust and sew to place the upper brim covering, turning the edge over the edge-wire of the frame and sewing it

to the underbrim. Next, adjust the top crown interlining turning edge down to the side crown and sew it to place. Cut away any extra fullness by cutting out small gores. Finally turn in the edges of the side crown interlining and place it about the side crown of the frame. It will overlap at the back, $l/2$ inch, where it is sewed to the frame.

To Place the Velvet Covering.

Slash the upper brim covering about the headsize to the depth of a scant $¥l$ inch and slip it aver the crown. Make the middle front coincide with the middle front of the brim. Pin the front, back and sides to place at the brim edge and base of the crown, smoothing, but not stretching, the fabric to the frame. Turn the edge down over the edge-wire and sew to the interlining, cutting out any superfluous material. In smoothing the velvet, care must be taken to avoid stretching it on the bias of the goods. Fig. 4 shows the upper brim covering partly sewed to place in this interlining. In sewing, the needle is slipped under the edge of the velvet and then in the interlining. The slashes about the crown are next sewed to the side crown with a long stitch on top and a short one on the inside of the crown, using the "stab" stitch.

The facing is next adjusted as shown in Fig. 5. After smoothing and pinning the velvet to place, the edge is turned in all around and neatly "slip-stitched" to the upper brim covering. Any surplus material must be trimmed away.

To Slip-Stitch the Edge.

Hold the underside of the hat next to you, with the thumb and forefinger of the left hand. Use a small scrap of velvet to hold the hat, the pile side resting against the velvet covering. This prevents the velvet from being marred. Sew from right to left. Take a very short stitch in the velvet turned over the edgewire then slip the needle through the edge of the facing. The stitches will be invisible.

Having finished the edge, the headsize is to be cut out and sewed to the inside crown in the same way as described for the interlining. The top crown is next adjusted and sewed to the interlining as shown in Fig. 6. In adjusting the side crown covering, one end is first sewed to the interlining of the hat. After smoothing the covering around the side crown (with upper and under edges turned in) the remaining end has its edge turned in and is slip-stitched to place.

LESSON XI.

How to Make Folds.

Folds are made of various jfabrics, from strips, cut on the bias. To make perfect folds it is essential that the strips be cut on a true bias. Fig. 1 illustrates the method of finding a true bias. The fabric is laid on the work table and the straight end, designated by the line "A-C," is folded back *Fig. I*

Method of finding a true bias and of measuring a length having one straight and one bias end.

so that the edge lies along the selvedge of the goods, designated by the line "A-B." When the material is cut along the line "A-D," a true bias edge is made on the material and on the piece cut away. Fig. 1 shows also the method of measuring a length of material having one bias and one straight end. Its length is determined by measuring from a point at the middle of the bias edge "A-D" (designated by "E"), to the middle of the straight edge (designated by "F"). Having cut a true bias edge, strips are to be cut from which to make the several kinds of folds. After the width of the required strips is determined, mark the fabric along each selvedge with chalk, or notch it. Fold the fabric on the line connecting these markings and cut along the fold. If the strips are to be quite narrow, it is best to draw a line with chalk as a guide for cutting. When velvet is to be cut the chalk line should be drawn on the back of the material. When the strips are cut, they are joined by machine-stitching or back-stitching the ends together after trimming away the selvedge. The seams should be laid flat open and may be sewed open with a feather stitch.

Pipings.

A piping or piping fold is simply a bias strip folded along its center, lengthwise, with its raw edges brought to gether and overcast or basted down. Such folds, or pipings, are used in joining seams, finishing edges and covering surfaces.

A Plain Fold.

In Fig. 2 the fold known as a "plain" fold is illustrated. To make it, cut a bias strip twice as wide as the finished fold is to be. Bring the raw edges together and use the

Fig. 3

French or Milliner's Folil. saddlers' stitch or the cross-stitch to hold them. Stitches should not be drawn tight in joining the edges of the folds.

The Milliner's or French Fold.

In Fig. 3, a milliners or French fold is shown. To make this it is necessary to cut a strip twice as wide as the finished fold is to be plus i inch for turning under at one edge. Fold the lower edge of the strip up on the wrong side of the material. One-third of the width of the strip folded up, leaves one-third remaining to be folded down.

Turn the raw edge under to the depth of y inch and fold this portion down. Slip-stitch this edge to the material under it as shown in Figure 3.

Double French Fold.

Figure 4 illustrates the double French fold. This fold requires a strip four times the width of the finished fold. Make first a plain fold. Double this fold lengthwise, that is, bring the fold edges together, folding the stitches in.

Turn back the top fold one-third of its width. This will give a little fold through the center. Slip-stitch this down concealing the stitches, and those used in making the plain fold as shown in Fig. 4.

Folds are sometimes lined with muslin. Where a rolled effect is desired they are rolled over cord. There is nothing in millinery more universally used than folds and to cut, make and adjust them correctly is considered a test of millinery workmanship.

LESSON XII.

Bindings and Facings.

Having learned, how to make folds the pupil must proceed to learn to apply her knowledge to the various methods of finishing brims. The most common method in use is that of binding the brim with a plain bias fold. After the body of the hat is covered, the edges of the covering are trimmed off even with the edge wire, and sewed down by overcasting the edgewire all around. A plain bias fold is then made, of any desired width to be used as a binding. A narrow binding is easier to adjust than a wide one.

Having made the fold one end is pinned over the edge at the back and the fold stretched along the edgewire. It should be pinned at intervals until it is placed entirely around the brim. After smoothing the fold to the brim until it is a snug fit, the free end is cut off on the bias to proper length. A portion of the binding is then unpinned and slipped off the brim. The bias ends are sewed together with a back stitch and the fold readjusted. A few slip-stitches, about the brim edge will hold it to place permanently.

A pretty finish, is made by binding the frame with *a* narrow bias strip before it is covered. When the outside covering has been placed, the edges of the upper and under brim are turned under and slip-stitched to the binding, which thus forms a piping about the brim.

A beautiful, finish is made by stretching a wide bias strip about the brim edge without turning in its raw edges. These are covered by a narrow French or double French fold slip-stitched to place.

Folds may be laid in parallel rows on the upper or under brim edge. For this finish the edge is first bound with a bias strip. Three or four piping folds are then placed each one slightly overlapping the preceding one. Over the raw edge of the last one, a plain or a French fold is slip-stitched, as a finish.

Fancy Facings of Folds.

There are many fanciful ways of finishing brim edges by means of folds. Short pipings, are placed over the edge of the brim, from the base of the crown to the headsizes, each overlapping, slightly, the preceding one and given a straight or diagonal direction. The raw ends are covered by a plain fold slip-stitched to place at the base of the crown. Or a long piping fold is cascaded, back and forth, over the brim edge. This makes a very pretty effect, as the difference in direction of the pile in velvet gives the effect of two alternating shades.

Besides the various brim finishings of folds, brim edges are finished with narrow ruffles of lace or other materials and with shaped borders.

Shaped Borders.

Sometimes a border is desired about a brim, too wide to be made from a bias strip stretched to place. Such borders must be cut to fit. They are cut by a pattern in the same way as smooth facing. In addition to these there are various decorative finishes. But the pupil who has learned to finish brims by the methods described will be able to copy any others.

Facings.

Many hats, require facings. A facing is placed to cover the underbrim, as a finish, or to introduce a surface or color next the face unlike that of the body of the hat.

Facings are made of various materials namely braids, velvet, crepe, silk, satin, chiffon, malines, lace and ribbons, applied to underbrims in a variety of ways.

To Face the Hat With Braids

Beginning at the back the braid is to be sewed on row after row, as on the upper brim. For the heavier braids a stab stitch is used. Thrust the needle through the braid near its outer edge, to the upper brim. Here it is slipped under a tiny fiber or shred of the braid and then back to.the underbrim. This makes a small stitch, invisible or nearly so, on the upper brim. The needle is then thrust through the facing braid a half inch or a little less, from the first stitch, and a tiny stitch made on the facing braid. By thrusting the needle through to the upper brim again, the longer stitches are concealed under the braid.

Gathered Braid or Lace

Lace braids are frequently used for ruffled facings. They may be sewed to a facing, row after row, using an overcast or back stitch along the drawn edge. In this case the needle is thrust through the

mull covering of the frame. Narrow lace is put on in the same way, and these effects are especially good in children's millinery.

Fabric Facings

Velvet, satin and other fabrics are placed according to directions given in Lesson X. for facing a shape with velvet.

LESSON XIII.

Lace and Shirred Net Hats.

Hats of net, lace or similar fabrics are made over frames of fine silk covered wire. Frames made without tie-wire should be chosen as tie-wire ends catch in the mesh of these fabrics or show through them.

Laces, nets and similar fabrics are laid smoothly over frames or shirred to them. If the frame is to be covered smoothly it is usually best to place a foundation of maline or chiffon, (over which fine lace or net is placed) according to the directions given for covering a frame with mull.

To Cover a Hat With Lace.

Hats are covered with all-over lace in the same manner as they are covered with velvet when the lace is to be laid on plain. When the same kind of lace is used to cover both upper and under brim it is usual to place the figures in the pattern so that they coincide. That is, a leaf, scroll, flower or other design on the upper brim lies directly over the same design on the under brim. Edges of brims in hats of all-over lace, laid on smooth, are usually finished with a fold or border of velvet or other fabric.

In covering a crown with all over-lace, laid on smooth, the same methods are followed as those given for covering a crown with velvet. For a square crown the top crown piece is cut an inch greater in diameter than the diameter of the crown and laid smoothly over it. The half inch allowance all round is turned down and tacked to the side crown, the superfluous fulness either laid in plaits or cut away, A bias strip is cut an inch wider than the height of the crown if a sloping crown is to be covered. It is turned in *y2* inch along each edge and stretched about the side crown. A straight strip is cut for a

straight crown. Hats of lace or net laid smoothly to the frame are usually lined with net or chiffon.

Smooth Coverings of Wide Lace.

Frames are often to be covered with wide edgings or insertions or scarfs of lace laid on smoothly. In any instance the frame is first covered with a foundation of maline. Beginning at the middle of the back the strip of lace is sewed over the edge wire along its straight edge on the upper brim. When it has been sewed entirely around the frame it is turned over the edge wire and basted to the under brim about 1 inch in from the edge. Wherever extra fulness appears the mesh of lace is cut away from the figures. Having cut out all the superfluous fulness the figures are sewed, with small concealed stitches, to the maline foundation. This makes a smooth covering shaped to the frame without plaits or gatherings.

Crowns may be covered in the same way, which amounts to applying the pattern in the lace, after cutting away the superfluous mesh, to the foundation of maline or net previously placed over the frame. In Fig. 1 an under brim covering is shown of a lace edging laid on smoothly over a maline foundation by cutting away the mesh from the pattern. It is impossible to detect where the edges join and the lace appears to have been made to fit the frame.

To Cover a Crown with Wide Edging.

Two strips of edging are usually required to covur a crown. These strips are joined along the scalloped edges. This joining is done by one of three methods. The convex edge of a scallop on one strip is fitted into the concave edge of the scallop on the other strip and the two edges are sewed together. Or the scallops are tacked together at the middle of the edge of each one. Or the scalloped edges are joined by means of a narrow strip of net or a lace insertion to which both are sewed. After the strips are joined, the lace is stretched over the crown, which has previously been covered smoothly with foundation of maline or other fabric. Hats made of sheer embroidery in swiss, batiste, etc., are managed in the same way as those covered with lace. When heavy laces or embroideries are used they are often placed upon a frame without a foundation. Hats of these materials are classed as "Lingerie" hats.

To Cover Frames with Narrow Edgings.

Narrow laces are applied to frames in the same manner as braids. The frame is first covered smoothly with thin material to which the lace is sewed. Nearly all narrow laces are provided with a gathering string along the straight edge. The lace is adjusted to the frame by drafting the gathering thread and sewing the lace to the foundation along the gathered edge. The methods given in the lesson on covering the frame with braid are used for covering a frame with narrow laces.

Wide Edgings Extending over Brim Edge.

When it is desired to cover a frame with a wide edging and to allow the scallop to project beyond the brim edge, the lace selected should be wider than the width of the brim by as much as the depth of the scallop. If the lace is to be gathered on, once and a half to twice the circumference of the brim is the length allowed to give the requisite fulness. Heavy laces require little fulness and the heaviest are bought in plaques ready to adjust to the frame. Lace ends should be joined together by felled seams so that no ends will ravel out.

To Make a Felled Seam.

Bring the ends of lace together, allowing one end to project i/j inch beyond the other. Sew these ends together in a shallow seam. Fold the projecting edge over the other edge and turn the seam down along the line of sewing. Stitch the folded edge down with short slip-stitches. This sews the seam flat to the lace.

To Dispose Fullness Evenly.

When a wide edging is to be gathered to the frame to form a ruffle about the brim edge, the fulness must be disposed evenly. Having cut off the length of lace required fold it in the middle and mark the middle point with a pin. Find the middle of each half and make the point with a pin. This will quarter the length of the lace. Pin the middle of the strip to the middle front of the brim edge and pin the quarter markings to the middle of each side. Join the lace in the back with a felled seam and gather to the base of the crown and about the brim edge.

LESSON XIV.

Shirred Net Hats.

When frames are to be covered with shirred net, the first matter to consider is the cutting of the material. This may be cut on the bias, lengthwise or crosswise. The net is cut on the bias for making the softest frills about the brim edge.

viii Strips of Fabric Joined Kejuly for Shirring.

If it is desirable to avoid seams it is cut lengthwise. For economy and because of the pattern in the net, the material is frequently cut crosswise. When several strips must be joined together to make the requisite length they must be sewed in tiny felled seams.

The amount of net required to make a shirred hat, varies according to the sheerness of the net. Very fine nets require more material than heavier ones as greater fulness is necessary in applying them to the frame.

For a net of average thickness allow a strip three times the length of the circumference of the brim and tw'cc. as wide as the width of the brim at its widest part plus the allowance for the frill. For a double frill about the brim edge an extra allowance must be made equal to twice the width of the extra frill.

For covering the crown a strip of net must be allowed three times as long as the circumference of the base of the crown and as wide as the distance from the center of the crown at the top to its edge, plus the width of the side crown, plus one inch allowance for sewing and turnings.

In calculating the width of strips to be used for covering the brim or crown one must reckon with the several ways of applying shirred net to frames. If the net is to be shirred into flat casings for the wires no extra width is allowed, but if wires are to be inserted into tucks or raised cords, twice the width of each tuck must be allowed. In calculating the length of the heavier net, once and a half to twice the circumference of the brim is allowed and once and a half the circumference of the base of the crown.

There are three methods of making shirred net hats. By the first method the net is shirred over the wires of the frame so that each wire is encased by rows of shirrings. By the second method the shirrings are run in the net and the shirred fabric applied to the frame afterward without encasing the wires. By the third the net is shirred into casings, or casings are applied to it, and the wires run in afterward. The last method is seldom employed.

To Make a Shirred Hat by the First Method.

Select a plain frame of fine wire, made without tie-wire, and measure the circumference of the brim. Select a net of average thickness and cut from it, on the bias, two or three strips twice as wide as the brim plus two inches for the frill, plus one inch allowance for turning into headfize. Sew these strips together in narrow felled seams, as shown in Figure 1, making a strip three times as long as the circumference of the brim and joining the ends with a felled seam. Fold the circlet thus made lengthwise along the center, with the seams inside, and all turned one way. Fasten the thickness together with pins and divide the circlet into quarters, marking each quarter with a cross stitch of thread as shown in Figure 2. The markings are indicated by small crosses. At the width of the frill from the folded edge, run a silk shirring thread around the circlet. Adjust the net over the frame, placing the quarter markings at the middle of the front, back and each side of the outer edge wire and pin or tack the net to the wire at these points. The net is now placed ready for shirring with one section over the upper brim and the other over the under brim. Now draw up the shirring thread already placed and dispose the fulness evenly about the edgewire. Next pin the two thicknesses of net together at intervals just inside the edge wire.

Place a few running stitches in the net close up to the wire and through both thicknesses and draw these stitches up to form a casing for the wire. The wires are encased this way all around the frame. The needle runs from right to left, taking up an inch of the fabric at a time. After en casing the edge wire, the net is pinned about the stay wires and shirred in the same manner. Figure 2 shows this process of shirring the net to the frame.

Cut the net for the crown, forming a strip three times as long as the circumference of the base of the crown and as wide as the distance from the center of the top crown to its base, measured over the edge of the top crown. Allow one inch extra for sewing and turning into the crown. Having made the circlet for the crown, run a shirring thread within a quarter inch of one edge, draw this shirring thread up as tightly as possible to form the center of the crown. This forms a plaque of the net. Sew the center of the plaque to the wires at the center of the top crown with the seams inside. Pin the plaque to the edge of the top crown at the middle of the front, back and sides and run in a shirring thread to adjust the net to the top crown wire. Tack the shirred net to the wire at intervals of a half inch all around. Turn the allowance over at the base of the crown and run in a shirring thread encasing the base wire in the net. If the frame is in one piece it will be necessary to slash the net at each brace wire as the shirring thread reaches it.

Shirring threads may be run in to follow each stay wire if desired. It is sometimes required to cover both the brim and crown with one piece of net. In this case the width of the necessary strip is calculated by adding to the width allowed for the brim, the height of the side crown plus the radius of the crown, plus one-half inch for sewings and turnings.

Shirred Net Hats with Tucks

Net is sometimes applied to the frame with tucks along the casings. In this case extra width is allowed for tucks on one or both sides of the brim and on the crown. The process is the same as that just described except that a tuck is laid in the net along each casing' and run in by the first thread used for the casing. Or tucks are run in between the casings as shown in Figure 3, before the net is adjusted to the brim.

Shirred Net Hats in Which Wires are Not Encased.

For shirred hats in which the wires are not encased the brim is covered with a strip of net in which shirred tucks have been previously run. To make such a brim a strip of material wide enough to allow for tucks is prepared by the method already described. The shirring thread is run in the frill about the edge and as many tucks as are required are run in the fabric before it is adjusted to the brim. After pinning the strip to the brim, according to the directions already given, the shirring threads are pulled up and tied. adjusting the coverings to the brim. The fulness is evenly disposed about the brim-edge and the fabric tacked at intervals to the edge-wire. It is then gathered into the hea'1. size at both upper and under brim coverings and sewed to the head-size wire. *mg.* 6 *rig.* 7

When a double frill is desired about the edge the process differs a little at the start from that given for a single frill. An extra allowance in width must be made equal to twice the width of the extra frill. The circlet made for covering the brim is folded lengthwise *with the wrong side out,* as shown in Figure 6, and the two thicknesses of material is next turned right side out and the two frills laid so that the stitching on the inside forms the base of each. By this method a double frill is made as shown in Figure 7.

Third Method for Making Shirred Hats.

Hats of net, embroidery, mull, thin silk and similiar fabrics are sometimes made by running casings in the shaped material and afterwards inserting wires or reeds. This method is suited to that class of hats called "tub" hats which, as their name implies, may be taken apart and washed. In hats of this character there are no brace wires and the fabric must be depended upon,. with the help

of the inserted wires to hold the hat in shape.

In cutting materials into strips for hats of this kind they are not cut on the bias, but either lengthwise or crosswise. Heavier fabrics made into sun hats or bonnets are provided with casings set on in which willow reeds or wires are inserted. Hats of this character are made for children. The wires or reeds may be slipped out of the casings, the fabrics laundered and the wires placed again. These wires or reed supports are made sufficiently long to overlap one inch at their ends. Here they are sewed or wound and tied together. Openings are left in the casings in which to insert them.

Nearly all hats of this character are made with soft tam crowns. Heavy fabrics such as pique, embroidered cambric, etc., are cut into shape for brims and crowns and afterwards furnished. with casings. Crowns are rarely wired and are either sewed or buttoned to the brim.

The major portion of lingerie are made by one of the methods described in this lesson.

LESSON XV.

Mourning Millinery.

There are special kinds of millinery used for special purposes. The most important of these are the hats and bonnets made for wear during periods of mourning.

Fabrics for Mourning Millinery.

Specially woven fabrics are used for making mourning millinery. Among them the best known are crape, mourning silks, nun's-veiling, bombazine, silk grenadine, uncut velvet, felt, dull finish taffetas, chiffon and novelty materials having a deep rich black color and dull luster. Of these the fabric used exclusively for mourning. is crape.

Shapes for Mourning Hats.

In selecting shapes on which to make mourning millinery, extremes of size must be avoided. Shapes should be medium in size and inconspicuous. The featherweight buckram shape or those of rice net and wire are.most convenient for mourning millinery.

Making of Mourning Hats.

In the making of mourning millinery, workmanship counts for more in this branch than in any other. It is therefore necessary for the pupil to first master the making of folds, cords, tucks and pleats, as these form the largest part of the trimming and bodies of mourning hats.

Crape is a material having a "rib" running diagonally across its surface. That is, the surface is covered with broken ridges all running in a diagonal direction. The ridges run from left to right when the crape is laid right side up on the table.

Making Folds of Crape.

In making folds of crape the student proceeds by the method given in the lesson on "How to make folds", except that the strips from which crape folds are made are usually cut on the straight as the rib runs diagonally across the material, that is on the bias of the weave, it is obvious that strips cut on the bias will either follow or cross this rib. The fold made from such a strip will show the rib running lengthwise on or straight across the fold. When it is desired to have the rib run diagonally across the fold the strips must be cut *on the straight of the material.* In Figure 1, a cord is shown covered with a strip of crape cut on the straight of the goods.

A soft cotton cord, called cable cord, is used for making crape covered cords. Strips of crape are folded over them and the edge sewed together. When the rib is to run parallel with the fold or cord, the crape is to be cut on the bias. In Figures 2, 3 and 4, folds are shown made of crape.

Making Tucks.

Tucks are made by basting plaits in a fabric and stitching them. They are usually placed in parallel rows and are uniform in width. They may be varied in width however. If they are placed in groups in which they gradually increase or diminish in width, they are said to be graduated.

To make tucks, therefore, it is necessary to first lay the material in a plait of uniform width, and baste this plait to place. Finally sew the plait in the material. Remove the basting threads and press with a warm iron on the wrong side.

Tucks are sewn in by hand or by machine stitching. The runing stich is used with an occasional back stitch introduced to hold the sewing firmly.

Plaited Materials.

A series of folds, placed at regular intervals and uniform width, pressed, or otherwise made to stay in the material, constitutes a plaiting. Materials are plaited by hand or by one of the various plaiting machines which are made for this purpose.

There are several varieties of plaits, including the box plait, double, single or quadruple boxplaits, side plaits, knife plaits and "sun" plaits. The side, and box plaits are often used in mourning millinery.

To Make Plaits.

To make a side plait lay a fold in the material as wide as desired (say one-half inch) and baste it in using a measuring rule to keep the width uniform for the length of the plait. Along the line of basting, the outside edge of the next plait will lie. At a distance from this line, of three times the width of the first plait, mark a line on the fabric, with a fine basting thread or tiny pencil mark. This marks off the amount of material and space needed for the second plait. Fold the second plait in the material, keeping it, by measuring the same width as the first, and basting' it along the line already marked. Continue this process until the required number of plaits have been laid in the material. They are usually pressed into the material by covering the plaited surface on the wrong side, with e. damp cloth and ironing with a moderately hot iron. Plaits may be tacked or blind-stitched down where pressing will not answer the purpose. Plaiting machines may be used for nearly all fabrics.

To Make Box Plaits.

A boxplait is formed by making two plaits of the same width and turning them in opposite directions. Double, triple or quadruple boxplaits, as their names indicate, are made by forming second, third and fourth plaits back of che first one formed. They may or may not be of the?ame width as the first plait. Triple and quadruple plaits are used for making ruchings. Single and double boxplaits are used in draping mourning veils and for other purposes.

To Make a Double Box Plait.

Lay the material in a plait, as for a sideplait, and baste down. Lay a second plait of the same width over the first and baste down. Lay a third plait, turning it in a direction opposite to the others. Baste this down; under this plait lay a fourth like it, basting to place. Tack with needle and thread, or press on the wrong side and remove bastings.

Besides folds, tucks and plaits, there are some fanciful forms into which crape is made up for mourning millinery. These are usually formed from folds.

Rosettes of folds, crape foliage, fruits and ornaments may all be fashioned by the milliner. The even, neat appearance resulting from the use of folds, tucks and plaits, make them the foundation for the work of making, mourning millinery.

Bonnets and Toques.

Bonnets are made on buckram or wire shapes that fit the head more or less closely. The shapes are varied by the addition of small brims or coronets. A coronet brim is a shaped piece of buckram, rice net or wire which is added to the cap-like crown, about the edge, and which stands up like a coronet.

A Toque is small or medium-sized shape, between a bonnet and a turban in outline. These and the smaller hat shapes, including turbans, are usually chosen for first mourning, and veils are worn with all of them.

To Make a Bonnet.

Select a buckram shape, for a bonnet which is simple in outline.

Cut out a tissue paper pattern by placing a square of tissue paper over the crown and folding the superfluous paper about the edge of the bonnet into plaits. Cut away this extra paper and then trim the pattern to follow the outline of the bonnet-edge. This will give you a pattern having gores (small triangular pieces) cut around the e.:e. Place this pattern on a small piece of black sheet wadding and cut the wadding out by the pattern, allowing one-fourth of an inch extra about the edge. Place the piece of wadding thus cut out over the buckram shape, in the same position a's that in which the pattern lay. Smooth and gently stretch the wadding, where necessary to make it conform perfectly to the shape.

After the shape has been covered with wadding in this way the material to be used is to be stretched over this and sewed to place. Turn one corner of the fabric down and cut it away to form a bias edge. Pin the middle of this bias edge to the bonnet frame at the middle of the front. In forming the bias edge, on a piece of crape, fold the material back so that the bias edge will cut across the rib at a right angle.

Having pinned the fabric to the wadding covered frame, at the front stretch, and smooth it to the shape, pinning it down to place about the edge. It may be necessary to lay a few plaits about the shape near the edge, but the covering should be fitted on by stretching the fabric, if possible. After the covering is placed thus, trim it off even with the edge of the shape. Sew the material down about the edge, overcasting it about the edge of the frame, and remove the pins. Stitches should be short and placed at intervals of a J4 inch all about the edge, to hold the covering smoothly to place.

The edge must now have a neat finish. Cut a bias strip of crape two and a half inches wide and make a plain fold. Stretch the fold about the edge of the bonnet and slip stitch it to place. Use a fine needle and silk thread and do not draw the stitches tight enough to show in the fold. The bonnet shape is now covered and bound. It may be lined and draped with a veil without further preparation or decoration, but it is usual to finish the edge with several folds or cords or some other arrangement of the crape.

Bonnet With a Finish of Folds.

Cover the bonnet and bind the edge with a bias strip (not a fold) of crape. This strip should be one inch wide. Cut a second bias strip two inches wide, to make the first fold about the edge of the 'bonnet. Cut this strip four inches longer than the first strip cut. The ends of this fold are to be used to conceal the raw ends of the succeeding folds which are to be placed about the bonnet.

Beginning midway in the length of this strip sew one half of it to the bonnet, starting at the middle point of the front of the shape. Sew the strip smoothly near the edge of the bonnet, with the right side of the fabric down, and with the greater part of the strip projecting beyond the edge of the bonnet. Use the stab stitch, placing a short stitch on the inside of the bonnet and a longer one outside. (This longer stitch should be about one-quarter to one-third inch in length). Then sew the other half of the strip to the bonnet. Two inches are left free at each end.

Placing the Folds in the Frame. Cut three bias strips, each, one and one-half inches wide and fold each strip lengthwise along the center, basting the raw edges together. When the folds have been prepared in this way, place one of them with its folded, or outer, edge over the raw edges of the strip just sewed to place. The ends of this fold meet at the middle of the back and are trimmed squarely off at the point. Place the second and third folds in the same way, sewing all to place and trimming the ends where they meet at the back. Cover the edges of the last fold placed with a tiny French fold made of a bias strip of the material, two inches wide.

When all the folds are placed in this way the raw edges of the first strip, which projects beyond the edge of the bonnet, is to bs turned in a tiny hem and sewed to the edge of the bonnet on the outside of the shape. Use a fine needle and silk thread. The slipstich must be used.

The extra length at the ends of this strip forms the folds which conceal the raw ends of the other folds. Turn under the ends of these finishing folds and sew them down firmly to the bonnet, concealing the stitches.

A bonnet covered and finished in this way is meant to be worn with a veil and needs only to be lined to complete it. Sometimes a ruche is worn in the bonnet. This ruche is a fold of white crape or crape-like material.

To Line the Bonnet.

Cut a circular piece of silk or other lining fabric from four to five inches in diameter, and paste or sew it in the crown of the bonnet. Cut a strip of the same fabric four inches wide and long enough to extend about the edge of the bonnet. Allow one inch extra length for turning under at the ends. Hem the lining along one edge with a half inch hem. Sew the lining in, beginning at the middle of the front and sewing first one half and then the other. Turn under the ends and cut a tiny slit in the hem at the turning. Insert a baby ribbon in this slit, run it through the hem and out of the slit at the other end. Draw up the lining and tie in a very small flat bow.

Covering the Coronet.

When the bonnet has a coronet, this is covered with folds laid on in a variety of ways or with crape or other fabrics, made into fanciful forms. A favorite method is to alternate crape folds with those of other fabrics used for mourning wear. A pattern should be cut of the coronet and an outer lining of wadding placed, if the covering fabric is to be stretched on plain. If the coronet is to be covered with folds or other forms into which mourning materials are fashioned the sheet wadding may be omitted, but in this case the coronet is to be covered with the material or with a foundation for the material, such as thin silk.

When very soft, thin fabrics are used it is sometimes necessary to use a supporting material, as a lining, to produce neat effects.

In this particular branch of millinery certain rules may be followed by the student, insuring her success in making mourning hats.

Rules for Making and Trimming Mourning Millinery.

1. Shapes selected for mourning wear should be moderate size and conservative as to the style, that is, not in the extreme of the prevailing modes. They should not be eccentric or unusual in design.

2. Crape in black or white should be selected for deep mourning. Deep mourning is the mourning apparel used by adults immediately after the death of a near relative (and for a definite period of time thereafter). 3. Crape may be used in combination with other mourning fabrics at the discretion of the wearer for first mourning. Such combinations are correct. 4. Materials suited for mourning millinery are those which have a deep black or pure white color, with soft or dull luster. LESSON XVI.
The Mourning Veil.

Mourning veils are made of crape, nun's veiling, or grenadine, net and of other fabrics, which are usually bordered with crape. They may be bought with woven-in borders. Many people prefer a veil made from the piece-goods and hemmed or otherwise finished by hand.

To Hem a Crape Veil.

Decide upon the length of the veil (which may vary from a yard to almost two) and upon the width of its hem at the top and bottom. A hem from six to twelve inches in width is an elegant finish for the bottom and from three to four inches is appropriate for the top. Measure from the bolt sufficient material for the veil, allowing for hems and one inch more for turning in and making true, straight edges at ends.

True, Straight Edges.

The ends must be perfectly straight before the hems are sewed in. This is accomplished by drawing a crosswise thread from the material and trimming along the line made in this way. Trim each end of the veil, by this method and draw a second thread at each end, marking twice the width of the desired hem from the end. Turn the end over one-half inch and baste it down to the wrong side of the material. This turned in edge is then laid on the second marking (made by the drawn thread) and basted to position with loose long stitches. The hem is then slip stitched, to place. The basting stitches are afterward cut and pulled out and the hem pressed with a warm iron, under a thickness of tissue paper or cloth.

A Second Method.

A second method for wide hems is very successful, making the appearance of a finished hem on both sides of the material.

After trimming one end of the fabric as just directed, measure off twice the width of the desired hem. Draw a thread from the material here and along the. line of the drawn thread, run in a basting, using white thread. This basting is to serve as a guide.

Begin at the other end and roll the veil carefully and evenly until the basted line is on the top of the roll. (See Fig. 1 If desired this can be done over a broom handle or curtain pole.

Bring the line up to the raw edged end of the veil and pin in a seam through three thicknesses. (See Pig. 2) Sew along the pinned seam fastening securely at the ends. It will be observed that the rolled portion is now enclosed in a double hem. (See Figure 3.) The next important step is to turn the hem right side out and at the same time to bring the veil out of its length. To do this first of all slip the pole out at one end of the hem. Then slip the finger in the hem, catching at one end and draw the material out.

The hem should be pressed with a slightly heated iron. The instructions, together with illustrations, show plainly the method of hemming in this simple and satisfactory manner.

Finishes for Mourning Veils.

Sometimes veils are finished in scallops around the edges. Scallops are accurately cut in the material and bound with tiny bias folds of crape. Embroidery silk is employed also to buttonhole the edges of scallops. Small straight folds are used to finish crape veils and other mourning veils. Folds for finishing should be cut on the bias when they are to be applied to curved lines, in order that they may lie smoothly.

Net Veils.

Net veils are finished with borders of crape or other fabric. These are folds, more or less wide, which are applied as a binding' to the veil. It is difficult to hem a veil of coarse mesh net hence the borders of crape, grenadine, ribbon, etc. A net veil may be hemmed and the top

of the hem finished with a fold of crape with narrow ribbon, such as grosgrain, or ribbon woven for the purpose. Veils are often finished with an embroidered design above the hem.

Draping the Veil.

Veils are draped on the hat or bonnet by means of small black pins with dull black heads. Two things are to be kept in view in draping the veil, in order to do the work successfully: the weight of the veil is to be evenly distributed (when it requires consideration) and lines resulting from draping should be long and almost unbroken. By keeping these points in mind the exercise of individual taste is possible.

Principal Methods.

In the shawl drape one corner is folded back to any desired depth, forming a triangular, partly double veil, to be pinned to the bonnet or toque. It is usual to lay the veil in a box plait along the bias edge formed by folding for the shawl drape. A wide double or triple box plait will be found to distribute the weight of a veil evenly.

To Make the Box Plait.

After folding over one corner to the desired depth pin the two thicknesses of veiling together and find the center of the bias edge. Mark the center with a pin or stitch. Lay a double box plait (at the center) about five inches wide and baste to place. Next pin the veil to the bonnet or toque and remove the basting. To throw the greater part of the veil toward the back it will be necessary to lay a triple, instead of a double box plait. The pins inserted to hold the veil to the toque will also serve to hold the plaits in place.

When the veil is adjusted to fall over the face, it is to be divided into two sections, marking the division with pins. That portion having the wider hem falls to the back and may be a little longer than the portion falling forward over the face, or of the same length. After marking the division with pins, spread the veil on a table and fold it along the center, lengthwise. Run a basting thread along this lengthwise fold to mark it. This is a guide line for making either side plaits or a box plait in the veil. Lay plaits and pin them down for a distance of three inches on each side of the crosswise division.

To Adjust the Veil.

Place the hat or bonnet on a head and place the veil over it so that the center of the plaits will coincide with the center of the crown. Pin the plaits to place at the base of the crown at the front and back. Remove the bastings and pins not required for holding the veil to the bonnet.

The veil is often used to drape the hat as well as to fall over it. One corner is pinned to the hat at one side by a bar pin or other ornamental pin of dull jet or of a form covered with crape. The veil is brought about the shape which it is arranged to cover wholly, or in part. The remaining length is laid in a plait falling from the back.

White fabrics as well as black are now considered correct for mourning and are made up according to the directions given in this lesson.

LESSON XVII.

General Instructions in Bow Making

According to Webster's Dictionary a bow is, "an ornamental knot with projecting loops formed by doubling a ribbon or string." In millinery a simple bow is a tied bow having two loops and two ends, such as one makes when tying a shoe string. The word bow, as used by milliners, includes many forms of ribbon garnitures, rosettes, knots, choux, in fact, nearly all decorative arrangements of ribbon. The Art of Expression.

As soon as the student has grasped the idea that the ability to give expression to bows constitutes the first essential of the art of bow-making, she will have a working basis from which to proceed. Bows are characterized as "saucy" "drooping," "rich," "buoyant," "limp," and other suitable adjectives, the descriptive words revealing what the bow expresses. They are also designated as, "skimpy," "sloppy," "crude," and "ugly," when they are badly made, thus demonstrating that the bows have expression and therefore character.

Harmony of Design and Weave. The relation between fabric and design must also be comprehended. If a "buoyant"

or "crisp" bow is required, one must choose taffeta or other ribbon having the requisite stiffness. Drooping and crushed bows are to be made of soft. pliable ribbons. In bows of brocaded ribbons, scant fullners is required. This' would be flat and uninteresting in bows of plain weaves, where one must use an abundance of ribbon. Heavy weaves, in rich deep lustres, made up for matronly wearers, are out of place in pert little bows designed for children. The student will soon discern the fitness of certain weaves of ribbon for certain effects.

Methods of Making.

Bows are either tied, sewed, or made with tie-wire. They are therefore designated by their terms as "tied," "sewed" or "tie-wire" bows.

Loops are designated as so many inches "deep." A loop four inches deep requires eight inches of ribbon to make it, as it is simply that length of ribbon doubled. A loop may be flat, but is usually gathered or plaited at its "base." Where the bases of the loops join and are covered by the knot, is the "waist" or "heart" of the bow. Ends are described by the manner in which they are trimmed, as "square," "round," "pointed," "clipped" and "diagonal". They are sometimes hemmed.

Sewed Bows.

Fig. 1 shows the method of forming loops. When plaiting ribbon for loops, pinch it down to its smallest compass, then sew firmly. Next plait in ribbon a distance from this point twice the length of the desired loop.

Bring this portion to the plaits already laid and sewed together, or wind thread about them and fasten with a few stitches. In making a tie-wire bow, the plaits are laid in, or the ribbon is crushed or pinched into a small space and tie-wire is wound about it to hold it in place. The ends of the wire are twisted and clipped when the loop has been formed. It is necessary to cut ribbon into lengths for ordinary millinery bows. A series of loops is made, as just described, and the bow finally completed by a knot at the heart.

Rosettes.

A rosette is a circular bow, or a series

of loops and ends arranged in circular form. Usually the loops are sewed, to make the rosette symmetrical. If consisting of a considerable number of loops or ends, these are sewed to a buckram foundation. This is a disc of buckram about as large as a silver dollar, for ordinary millinery rosettes. Innumerable fancy ribbon garnitures are classed as rosettes.

Staying Ribbon With Wire.

Sometimes it is necessary to stay ribbons with wire in order to hold them in required positions. A "ribbon wire" made especially for this purpose, consists of thin, flat tape, with tiny wire woven in its edges. This is blind-stitched to the back of the ribbon as shown in Pig. 2.

In Fig. 3 a small shiring wire is shown, which is inserted in a hem. This hem may be either made by hand or machine stitched. Usually a narrow hem, i inch in width, or less, is machine stitched over the wire.

Fig. 4 shows a third method of wiring ribbon, in which a heavy satin wire is buttonhole stitched to one edge. The wire should match the ribbon in color.

Trimming the Ends.

For a diagonal point have the scissors very sharp and trim the ends so that the angles at the points will be uniform. That is, if two or more ends appear, make them alike.

To trim in double points, or make "fish-tail" ends, fold the ribbon lengthwise and cut from the fold to the outer edge on a diagonal line. Rounded ends should be cut by a pattern.

Finally the student must learn to estimate the amount of ribbon necessary to make a bow of any sort. For loops, twice the depth of each one must be allowed, and a little leeway for the making.

For the hearts of bows only practice will enable the student to calculate accurately the length of ribbon required. Four to five inches is about the average length for wide-ribbons. After calculating the amount required for loops, add that required for ends, plus that required for the heart.

LESSON XVIII.

Baby Bonnets.

The simple little bonnet known as the "Stuart" cap, is the model chosen for young infants. Bonnets for later wear during babyhood are developed on this cap as a foundation. It is a simple affair made of two pieces of material shaped by a pattern to fit the head. Pig. 1 illustrates the diagram from which a pattern may be cut. The size of the bonnets will vary with the size of the heads for which they are made.

Flg. l Diagram for Stuart Cap

When making a bonnet to order it is necessary to measure the head in order to cut a cap to fit it. A pattern of the right dimensions should be cut. The diagram shown is designed for a pattern which will make a bonnet of medium size. Bonnets for babies, after the first few months, are made with little ruffles and capes to protect the face and neck from the sun or weather. The diagram Fig. 1 shows the shape of these ruffles.

Before attempting to cut a pattern from measurements of the head, the student should draw and cut out patterns according to the dimensions given here. Use a piece of manila paper and make dimensions and shape like those of the diagram.

To Cut the Pattern.

Cut off a strip of paper 18 inches long and 6 inches wide. Fold this strip in the middle, crosswise and crease the paper. Mark the creases with a lead pencil to designate the center of the pattern. On one edge of this strip measure *iy,* inches from the center just marked, on each side and mark the points with pencil mark. This is the front edge of the bonnet, so that this pattern is for a boonnet having a front edge 15 inches long. On the opposite edge of the paper strip mark off a.length of 16 *y2* inches.

This edge is designated as the line "c-d" in the diagram. At a distance of 2 inches in from the middle of the back of the paper strip, draw a line parallel with the edge as long as the strip, that is 18 inches long. This is the line "o-n" in the diagram. Parallel with and *2y2* inches from it darw a second line 16 inches long. This is the line between the points marked "xxx" in the diagram. Draw the

curved lines from the front "a" to "o" and "b" to "n". Next draw the slanting lines "o-c" and "n-d" in the diagram. You have now drawn a pattern for the front piece of the bonnet, according to the diagram and need only to cut it out along the outlines.

The second piece is made by drawing on the paper a circle having a diameter of 4 inches. This forms the little center of the back or crown of the bonnet, and these two pieces constitute the pattern for a Stuart cap.

The patterns for a ruffle about the face and cape, are next to be cut. For the former, cut a strip 26 inches long and 3 inches wide. Slope one end gradually to the ends, at a point one inch from the opposite edge. Cut the ends, a slanting line as shown in the illustration. (See Fig. 1)

For the cape cut a sheet of paper 22 inches long and 3 inches wide. Cut one edge in a curved slope as shown in the diagram. This slope is not as gradual as that in the diagram for the ruffle about the face. In order to make this curve correctly, divide the strip of paper into quarters, lengthwise and mark the divisions on the edge with pencil marks. The curve is cut along the quarter sections at each end of the strip, the remainder of the edge is straight. Mark on your patterns the letters appearing in the diagram. The front edge of the body of Fig. 1 is designated as "a-b" the back at "c-d." The straight edge of the ruffle for the cape is designated "f-g." (See Fig. 1.)

To Make a Bonnet.

Select a half-yard of mull, India linen, silk or any thin fabric suitable for a bonnet or use a lining material for practice. Cut out the circle for the back of the bonnet next. Cut a bias strip from the material making it % inches in width. Form a piping by folding and basting this strip over a small cord. This piping is to be basted about the circle cut for the back of the bonnet. Sew the ends of the piping together in a tiny felled seam. The crown center is thus made ready for the front of the bonnet. Lay the pattern you have just cut on the material: the straight edges of the

pattern should coincide with crosswise straight lines of the fabric. Allow a half inch for seams and cut according to the pattern. Notch the material where the marks "xxx" occur in the pattern. In the piece cut for the front, the edges corresponding to those marked "o-c" and "d-n" in the diagram are joined in a narrow felled seam. Gather the back edge"c-d" on a gathering thread using short running stitches. Dispose the fulness evenly and baste the gathered edge to the edge of the circle which you have previously prepared with piping. Sew the seam just basted, firmly and neatly with short back stitches, trim it evenly and bind with a narrow tape or bias strip of mull. The crown is now inserted in the bonnet and only the finishing remains to be done.

The front edge and sides of the bonnet are hemmed and finished in a great many ways. Little ruffles of soft Val lace, very narrow and of scant fulness are often used. Or an embroidered band is sewed in a narrow seam to the

Fig. « Cap, Ruttle and Cape Completed.

front and turned back. All seams are to be felled or bound. The sides of the bonnet are finished in a tiny hern and the ties are sewed on. These are strips of mull, batiste or other sheer fabric, about 4 inches wide and 18 inches long, finished with narrow hems. Two sets are made for one bonnet in order that they may be frequently laundered.

To Make the Ruffle and Cape.

Cut the ruffle and cape from the material placing the pattern so that the straight edges lie on crosswise sections of the goods. Allow a half-inch for hems and seams and cut the material by the pattern, which should be first pinned to the fabric. Hem the curved edge of the ruffle and the straight edge of the cape and bind the other edges. Finish by "whipping," that is, sewing with small overcast stitch a narrow lace edging to the hem of the ruffle and cape. Fig. 2 shows the the cape ruffle and cape completed and ready to be joined. The ties are usually sewed to place after the bonnet is otherwise completed.

All raw edges must be turned in or

bound. For very young infants materials must be soft and fine. The fulness in ruffle and cape may be made by gathering threads or by small plaits laid in the material.

t

Bonnets for Older Children.

As the infant advances into little girlhood bonnets become more elaborate in construction and trimming. The shape is made from a pattern having a greater number of pieces. Bonnets for older children are made with face frills and capes and with puffed crowns. The crown piece is not a simple circle as in the Stuart cap, but is slightly longer than it is wide and narrower at the base than at the top. A diagram for such a bonnet is shown in Figure 3. This diagram shows the crown piece, the face frill, the crown band, the full puff around the crown and the lining for the crown.

Bonnet for Older Child

Draft a pattern on manila paper according to the dimensions given in the diagram, cutting the pieces designated as a lining for the side crown and puff separately. Write on each piece (as shown in the diagram) designating the part of the bonnet it represents. Letter the pattern according to the letters in the diagram. Thus the piece marked "lining for side crown and puff" is lettered "a," "b," "c," "d." These letters are to appear on the pattern in the same position as shown in the diagram.

Select a soft wash silk for lining, and velvet, plush, silk or cloth for the bonnet; or for practice use calico or muslin.

Cut from the lining material the crown and piece marked "Lining for crown and puff" and sew the edge marked "c-d" in the pattern of the crown, placing the center of the edge "c-d" at the center of the top of the crown piece. In this crown piece the bottom edge is straight.

Sew the pieces together in a narrow seam and bind this seam with a narrow strip of the lining material so that it will not fray out.

Cut from the material for the bonnet the crown piece, puff and crown band. Baste these pieces to a piece of thin crinoline for interlining and cut the

crinoline like the bonnet: Gather both edges of the puff on a silk thread beginning at the center of the edge and running the gathering threads out to the ends. Tack the center of the edge marked "e-f" to the center of the top crown. Draw up the gathering threads, disposing the goods in scant fulness at the sides and greater fulness at the top crown. Sew the gathered edges to the crown using the short back stitch. A double gathering, that is, two rows of shirring, will dispose the fulness more neatly than a single row. Trim away the edge of the crinoline and bind the seam with a narrow bias strip of the lining silk. Gather the edge of the puff marked "g-h" in the same way and sew it to the crown band along the edge marked "k-1." Bind this seam.

You have now two little bonnets ready to sew together. Tack the lining bonnet inside the outside bonnet and turn in the raw edges of each, basting them down. Make a tiny fold or piping of the material of the bonnet by cutting bias strips 24 inch wide and folding them along the center lengthwise. Sew this piping inside the bonnet allowing it to protrude a little around the edge. Begin at the middle of the bottom of the crown piece. Use invisible stitches or machine stitch this piping to place with silk thread Matching the fabric in color. With short overcast stitches sew the edge of the lining (which you have already basted down) to the piping.

If the bonnet is to be finished with a little frill of lace about the face, this frill should be sewed to the piping before the piping is se,wed down. If greater warmth is required as in a bonnet for midwinter, introduce an interlining of Canton flannel or thin sheet wadding, cutting it like the silk lining.

Appropriate Trimmings.

The little bonnet may be trimmed in a great variety of ways with narrow or wide ribbon and with little bouquets of small flowers. In summer the same pattern Is used for batiste, mull and other summer fabrics, including lacy braids, nets and silk and Swiss embroideries.

The Face Frill.

The same bonnet with puffed crown

is often made with the addition of a frill about the face. The frill is cut by the pattern as shown in the diagram, with a thin crinoline used for stiffening and a silk lining. The three fabrics are basted together with the pile of the velvet (or the outside of the frill of other fabric used) turned in. The crinoline interlining and the silk lining are placed on it and all sewed together along the curved edge, on the sewing machine. The frill is then turned right side out and laid in single box plaits along the straight edge, beginning the plaits about three or four inches from the ends of the frill, at that part of the bonnet which is just about at the top of the ear. The frill is sewed in between the outside and the lining of the bonnet. A ruche about the face is basted after the bonnet is completed and may be removed and changed when soiled. Wide ribbon ties are used on these bonnets, as a rule, and may match either the bonnet or the lining in color. Such ribbon is also used in trimming them. .'.'.:. '.....' . :.

To Make Bonnets to Measure.

is not dm" uildren the bonnets will have to larger. It tottfa *sstJ?* meaSure for this bonnet" Determine the W

" m *th* rf W of the Straight Piece marked "crown band" TMS band extends from the Point of the

Jawon S an extends from the Pint of the thP mi,Ji 1? the same Position on the other, and from the middie of the top of the head to the forehead. The puff

WoDortTM11 Plef WiU have to be lengthened in the same proporhon as the band. They are also widened; the crown piece to cover the back of the head and the puff to stand up

Th. Vr,. lgMo Suit the individual taste. as ta, *1U..* ho has mastered the making of the bonnets almost 'I Lessons will find no trouble in making unon L £ to,nnet She may see, as these forms are those upon which others are built LESSON XIX.

Cutting and Sewing Furs.

The cutting and sewing of furs by professional furriers, are well systematized arts with their own technical terms.

Only a part of them need be mastered

by the milliner but a very necessary part. About the most difficult task set her is covering of shapes with fur in a workmanlike manner, the management of edges and of matching furs.

fig. i

The Only Tool
  Required In
  Cutting
  Furg.

Furs are cut with a furrier's knife (of which a drawing is shown here). It must be very sharp. Other instruments with fine sharp, thin blades and pointed at the ends, will answer the purpose, if a regular fur knife is not available. A good razor blade is a fair substitute.

The fur to be cut is laid on the table with the fur side down. The cutter makes an incision at the top of the piece to be cut, and runs the knife from the top downward, holding the top of the fur with the left hand. If the fur is to be cut in strips, the width is to be determined and lines drawn on the skin side to be followed with the knife. By cutting with a knife on the skin side the hair is not disturbed. It is pretty sure to be cropped and show a jagged edge if one attempts cutting with scissors.

Methods of Joining Furs.

Besides the straight-edge, there are three others commonly used by furriers in cutting furs to be matched and pieced together. They may be described as the "dovetailing" edges.

Fig. 2

Fur Cut iu Waved and Straight Edges.

They are cut in "waves," "saw-teeth" and tongues." The illustration shows them perfectly. The best edge to be used in any case is determined by the character of the fur, and the object of "dovetailing" is to make a joining of two edges imperceptible on the fur sides of the skins. It is often necessary to vary the width of the strip of fur on the skin side, in order to make the fur side uniform in width ijecattse'the hair is longer in some portions than in others.

The Furrier's Needle.

"In sewing the edges together by hand, a special needle, called by furriers a "finishing" needle, is to be used. It is a triangular needle, having three sharp edges merging into a sharp point. To do good work a needle of this kind must be used because an ordinary round needle pushes the hair through the skin and will not do neat and effective work. It requires more strength and takes more time also than a needle with cutting edges. Strong linen thread is used for sewing furs and the overcast stitch is used on nearly all the furs used for millinery purposes. A very shallow seam is made by holding the edges evenly together and overcasting the thread. The needle is thrust through very near the edges of the skin and the stitches set close together, that is at intervals of one-sixteenth of an inch. The thread is pulled tight. One of the most troublesome mistakes of the beginner is that of holding one edge a little fuller than the other, in sewing. In order to avoid this and the consequent bunglesome seam, the edges are to be tacked together at intervals of six inches before they are overcast. Another mistake of the amateur is in piecing without regard to the length of the hair in the two pieces to be sewed together with the result that the piecing is very perceptible instead of being invisible.

Nearly all furs used in millinery are thin skinned and not difficult to sew in an overcast seam. In piecing, the fur side is matched, and the skin side is cut in one of the four ways described in this lesson. As the task most often set for the milliner is that of using fur pieces (such as muffs and neckpieces that have become worn along the edges) to make or trim hats, she has the advantage of seeing the work of the professional furrier in piecing the skins and may ffuide herself by it.

To Cover a Frame with Fur.

If a hat frame is to be covered with fur, a pattern should first be cut from paper, by which to cut the fur covering. Do not allow extra width for seams, as the skin is to be dampened and stretched over the frame. In drying it shrinks and fits smoothly to place. If the task is simply to drape the frame with fur it is not so difficult.

Millinery furs are usually imitations of the skins for which they are called.

LESSON XX.

Preparation of Trimming for Hats.

Nearly all millinery trimmings require 'some, ssort of preparation before they can be placed on the hat. Ribbons flowers, feathers, bands and fabrics must be ready before they are mounted to the shape. The lesson on bow making will enable the pupil to manage ribbons.

Flowers as made by the manufacturer are branched in the most effective way. But when considered with relation to trimming the hat, must frequently be fashioned into other forms to meet the requirements of the styles prevailing That is, the branches require forming into wreaths, collars, rosettes, stick-ups, nosegays, etc. When stems are of wire they must be concealed or covered. Also, to remove strain from the hat they are sometimes first sewed to a foundation. hich is afterward sewed to the hat.

Flower Wreaths.

To make a flower wreath, select small sprays of flowers, or separate large bunches into their sprays. Measure off as length of large sized satin covered bonnet wire in green like the stem of the flowers (or in another color if necessary) as long as the desired wreath. With silk covered tie-wire wind the stems of the flowers and foliage to the bonnet wire neatly. Cut oif the stems of each spray allowing only sufficient length to hold it firmly to the bonnet wire. Place the sprays with a view to making the supporting wires as inconspicuous as possible. For wreaths of small flowers use small wires, satin covered shirring wire answers the purpose. Tie-wire should match the foundation wire in color.

In order to hold a wreath in a required pose on the shape, it 'is often necessary to provide supporting wires at inter"vals which attached to the wreath at one of their ends,.

and sewed to the hpt at the other. Satin covered shirring wire is used for this purpose selected to match the wires already used in making the wreath. The supporting wires are usually cut in lengths of about four inches, one end of which is wound about the large foundation wire and the other left free to be sewed to the hat and shortened, at the discretion of the trimmer. Four or five of such wires placed at equal intervals on the foundation wire are usually required for posing a large wreath. Many wreath effects may be bought ready for poking;?ome of these require the addition of supporting wires as jutt described.

To Form a Collar of Flowers.

To form a collar of flowers, first form a foundation of rice net or buckram by the method given in the Lesson on Bandeaux for making the foundation of a straight bandeau. Sometimes this foundation requires covering in which case it is to be covered in the same manner as the bandeau, using silk or ribbon instead of velvet. Sew sprays of flowers or single blossoms or petals to the foundation to form the collar.

To Form Rosettes of Flowers.

To form rosettes of flowers, foundations are prepared of buckram or rice net as for ribbon rosettes. Blossoms are sewed thickly to these foundations arranged in circles or in any manner the trimmer may fancy. Small circles of satin covered bonnet wire are covered with blossoms tied to them with tie-wire. Buckles, cabochons, quills, wings and plumes may all be simulated in flowers by making foundations of rice net bound with wire, sewing the blossoms to the foundat:on and covering the reverse side with silk.

Stick-ups are usually made by forming a foundation of large satin covered bonnet wire made into a narrow loop the length of the desired stick-up. Flowers are wound to this tie-wire cutting away any superfluous length of wire from their stems. At the base it is usual to wind the wire to the height of 2 inches with silk or velvet ribbon, sometimes finished in a little bow.

Little nosegays and bouquets are arranged and bound together with tie-wire. In these it is usual to feature the rubber stem as a part of the decoration.

How To Prepare Feathers.

Plumes and fancy feathers are provided by the manufacturers with wire stems in order that they may be posed at any angle. They are sewed directly to the shape or to a foundation of buckram or rice net which is afterward sewed to the hat. When sewed directly to the hat the wire stem must be concealed or covered in some way. It is usually covered by an ornament either made in the workroom or a manufactured ornament bought for the purpose. Or the stems are wound with silk or velvet ribbon. Small foundations of rice net cut any shape required, round, square or triangular, are bound with shirring wire and used for this purpose. After the stems of the feathers are sewed to them, the foundation is sewed to the shape.

How to Prepare Novelty Bands.

Novelty bands usually require wiring to form them into collars which can be effectively adjusted. Shirring wire inserted in a rolled hem along each side, and matching the band in color, is used for this purpose. Fabrics such as velvet and silk are used in drapery or cut into strips to be used instead of ribbon. They are used also to simulate wings and quills.

The Preparation of Fabrics.

When used in place of ribbon, fabrics are cut in strips and hemmed along the raw edges either by hand or machine stitching. Often a small wire is inserted in the hem to form a support. Sometimes raw edges are fringed or frayed as a finish. Ruchings of silk are effectively made with frayed edges. Velvet or silk ears are made by cutting two pieces of the fabric into the required shape and machine stitching the pieces together, right side in, around three sides. If a wire is needed for a support it maybe tacked about the seams or inserted after the ear has been turned right side out.

Fabrics are often shirred to form millinery ornaments. A collar is formed by shirring the fabric over the shirring wire at the top and bottom of the strip. Fanciful forms simulating flowers, wings, etc., are outlined with wire over which sheer fabrics such as lace, chiffon, etc. are shirred.

Ornaments of Braid.

Braids are used for making ornaments as well as for covering frames and making shapes. Ornamental braids are used for finishing the ornaments made of other materials. It is not usually necessary to support braids with a foundation of net. Braid ornaments are made by sewing the braid row on row into the shape desired and supporting the ornament by wire sewed to the under side. Thin lacy braids provided with a ruffling string are used to make innumerable ornaments, such as cabochons, buckles, rosettes and collars. Such ornaments are made by sewing the ruffled braid to covered foundations.

In fastening trimmings to hats they are both sewed and tied. Stong millinery thread in used knotted at the end. The needle is thrust through the hat from the underside and the thread drawn through alter, leaving a length of 3 inches free for tying. When the feathers or flowers or other ornaments have been sewed to place with several stitches the thread is tied in a hard knot on the under side of the hat and the ends clipped short.

Many ornaments are formed of folds which are sewed to foundations in the same.manner as braids.

LESSON XXI.

Trimmings Made in the Workroom.

Many millinery trimmings are made in the workroom, employing various materials in their construction. Among these, roses and other flowers, made of ribbon, velvet, silk, satin, lace, and gauze, metallic cloths and crape are used every season. Millinery braids are used in this way also. Buckles and other ornaments are made of millinery fabrics over rice-net or buckram foundations. Usually the fabrics are first cut into strips and made into folds. The folds are sewed to a shaped foundation to simulate wings, quills, ornaments, flowers and plumes.

Trimmings made in the workroom are especially appropriate for street hats and other special kinds of millinery, such as mourning hats and bonnets. For the latter crape provides the material for the body of the hat and also for its trimming.

Soutache braid makes very attractive trimming effects to be used on tailored hats. Ornaments simulating quills, feathers and flowers covered with millinery fabrics decorated with soutache or other narrow braids, are always good style. The Braid must be hand or machine stitched very neatly to the foundation form.

In the illustration which appears here, several trimming forms are pictured in which soutache braid is employed. By selecting one or more of these and making them according to directions given here, the pupil will learn something of the possibilities which lie in the use of narrow braids. Color combinations and the methods of sewing provide the essentials for consideration in getting these good results.

It is impossible in working diagrams to give any idea of beauty, but by following direction as to dimensions and color and by sewing the braids correctly, the ornaments will turn out perfectly, the outline drawings serving to show their form.

Soutached Wing Effect.

In Fig. 1 a Cupid wing is shown made of white corded silk. The wings were covered with braid put on in irregular "zigzag" fashion. The braid was sewed by hand on one edge with blind stitches, so that it stood up from the foundation. This method of sewing throws a shadow of the braid on the material of the background and gives results that cannot be obtained by sewing flat. The wing is 7% inches long, over all, 5 inches long from shoulder to tip, 3% inches wide at the shoulder and 1% inches across the base.

The foundation is of rice-net edged with fine or shirring wire. In the lesson on bandeaux the pupil has been taught how to make such foundations.

After making the rice-net form use it as a pattern and cut the silk, allowing three-quarters of an inch all around to turn over the edge of the foundation. Baste the covering to place and apply the braid. Use a fine needle and silk thread. Sew with a tiny stab or slip-stitch. After the braid is applied, line the wing with the same silk as that used for covering, allowing one-half inch to turn under when cutting the lining. Slip-stitch the lining to place. This wing and *some* other ornaments may have the covering machine-stitched in a casing

leaving an opening at the bottom and along one side sufficiently large to allow the rice-net form to be slipped in. Sew this opening together by hand afterward. In this case the stitches necessary to apply the braid will show on the back of the wing and the method is not to be used when the back of the ornament is visible on the hat.

Fig. 2 shows a large leaf or oval of cardinal red silk, made over a rice-net foundation by the method just described for Fig. 1. The braid in this ornament is sewed on one edge also, but in parallel rows set very close together. The entire leaf is covered in this way and a border of narrow fancy braid finishes it. Notice that the ends of each row of soutache are pushed through a tiny slash in the leaf.

Soutached Wing Trimming.

Figure 3 shows a wing for which the foundation is made in the same manner as those for Figures 1 and 2 and covered with satin in any color desired or in a heavy silk. Short lengths of Persian or other figured ribbons are available. The braid is applied in loops. Dimensions are as follows; Length, 14% inches; width, at top,.1 inch; width at center, 5% inches; at base; % inch; length of shorter half of wing, 10 inches.

Figure 4 represents an ornament made on a semi-circle of rice-net having a radius of 5% inches. Silk is laid in plaits forming rays from the center. The plaits are edged with soutache, which must be evenly and exactly disposed. It need not be sewed down in this ornaments but should be tacked at the base and edges of the semi-circle. Mercury Wings.

The cleverest of these little ornaments is shown in Figure 5. The ring is made on a buckram foundation. The small ,3 pair of wings are made on rice-net. The ring is covered with corded silk of which the wings are also made and lined. This ring is 4 inches in diameter and 2 inches wide. The small wings pass through the ring and are joined at the base. The wings are 5 inches in length from the tip to base. They are 3% inches wide at the center and 1% at the base. The soutache is sewed in

three standing rows, 1% inch apart. No. 6 consists of a cabochon covered with heavy white silk, on a light color, edged with three parallel rows of the braid, sewed on one edge as in the ornament just described. It is made over a buckram form 5% inches in diameter. A quill is thrust through two small slashes in the cabochon.

Black soutache is used on nearly all ornaments except in one-color hats. Braid matching the color of the trimming with which it is used is sometimes a better choice.

LESSON XXII.

The Art of Trimming.

In actual experience the learner in the workroom is put to copying hats before she essays trimming. In doing this work she absorbs, unconsciously, ideas which make it possible for her to become a trimmer after a time. Some of these ideas can be formulated and it is with these ideas or principles of the art of trimming that this lesson deals.

An inborn talent or "gift," as it is called distinguishes the great trimmer, as it distinguishes the real musician or the painter or the actress. This talent must be developed and brought out by practice. But there are some few rules and principles, which are as stable as those which govern in other arts, and which the student must absorb before she can make profitable headway by practise. »

Types of Hats.

The first thing to be learned by the beginner is the ability to distinguish between the different types or classes of hats. This is essential in order that she may govern her selection of trimming materials properlv.

They may be said to belong to three classes, broadly designated as "street," or "tailored hats," "trimmed" or "semi-dress" hats, and "dress" hats. "Picture" hats belong to the last class. Their names suggest their characteristics.

Th Tailored Hat.

Street or tailored hats are meant for utility and general wear. They are therefore properly made of substantial materials, in colors that are as nearly staple as possible. Their trimmings are selected with a view to withstanding wear, and such hats are plainer, than those intended for less public wear. These utility hats are trimmed with wings, quills, scarfs, ribbons, furs, fancy feathers, manufactured ornaments or ornaments made by the trimmer.

Good, durable braids or pressed straw shapes are chosen for these hats. Silk, felt and beaver, certain fabrics, and sometimes suede or other leathers are also employed in making the shapes.

Besides the well known trimming stuffs already mentioned, many novelties are manufactured each season for street hats. Simple familiar flowers, formed into rosettes are often used. In fact, it is not so essential to confine one's self to certain materials in making a selection for trimming street hats, as it is to know how to handle the materials selected, when placing them on the hat. Simple and durable trimming is proper for these hats.

The Dress Hat.

In selecting trimming for a dress hat, the fancy of the trimmer is not confined by the necessity for durability. The widest range is therefore allowed her choice. Flowers, no matter how fragile; colors, no matter how delicate, may be chosen. Everything within the field of trimmings is available,; ribbons, feathers, plumes, ornaments, embroideries, laces, furs, flowers, beads and the innumerable novelties which are prepared by the manufacturers each season.

All millinery fabrics are used in making the bodies of these hats, as lace, maline, chiffon, velvet, fur, silk and the whole range of straws and braids.

There is as great variety in shapes as in materials, ranging from the turban to the picture hat. The dress hat is made properly elaborate and made with grace and beauty uppermost in mind.

The Semi-Dress Hat.

The semi-dress hat is the hat which has to come to be classified as the "trimmed hat." Such hats are more elaborate than tailored hats, but the idea of utility enters into their making. They form the bulk of millinery stocks, as a rule, and all sorts of millinery materials «re employed in making them.

By visiting good displays of hats the student will soon learn to distinguish between "street," "semi-tiress" and "dress hats." These varieties are also designated as "tailored," "trimmed" and "pattern" hats.

The Simplest Form of Trimming.

The simplest trimming is in the form of a band, or collar of ribbon, or other fabric or material, placed about the crown of a hat. Such a decoration is appropriately used on all three classes of hats.

A simple collar or band placed about a crown may be finished by an ornament, a bow or a rosette placed at some point on its surface. This simple style of trimming is often designated as "severe," that is, it does not break up any line of the shape, or add anything to its expression.

The Functions of Trimming.

By the addition of a bow, rosette, feather or other trimming material, the lines of a shape may be changed, and adapted to the wearer's face. The student Will readily see, therefore, that the function of trimming, is, besides its decorative value, to *effect slight changes in form and afford grace* to the shape on which it is placed and to add to its becomingness.

Preserving the Outlines of the Shape.

The placing of Trimming should not conceal the outliae of the shape so as to destroy or contradict its lines. Too much trimming, or trimming badly placed, is worse than none. With regard to the variety of trimming to be used the rule is to use not more than three kinds on a hat. That is, one may use a ribbon, feathers and an ornament, or ribbon, flowers and an ornament, or flowers, foliage and lace, or any combination of not more than three materials. Great designers delight in simplicity in this regard. Simplicity does not mean meagerness of trimming, however. No hat can be beautifully trimmed if the trimming suggests "stinginess" in any way.

Preparing Trimmings for Street Hats.

The trimming for the street hat should be compact, well made, and selected, in good colors for general wear. Heading the list of colors are navy, marine, na-

tional and other good shades of blue. Hunter's and bottle green, emerald and moss greens, reds and some browns and plaids are especially useful and appropriate. The natural straw and "burnt" shades are most elegant and very durable, for straw hats which must be worn in all weathers.

No absolute directions can be given the student as to the selection of materials; good taste, which is a sense of fitness, must be exercised in each individual case.

You have now in mind what materials to select for trimming the three classes of hats which the milliner is ordinarily called upon to make.

Special Types of Hats.

Observation of millinery types soon impresses the student with the fact that each of the three classes of hats described is subdivided into groups. For instance, tailored hats include outing or tourists hats, distinguished by extreme simplicity in trimming and durability of materials. To this class belong hats for automobiling, and those designed especially for outdoor sports.

Semi-dress or trimmed hats include demi-season hats. In this class the materials selected belong to either warm or cold weather so that the hat is appropriate for the periods of transition from one season to another.

In the dress hat class are included evening and picture hats. In these, extremes of size and style and ultra ideas in trimming are appropriately used. There are three principles by which to guide the student in her attempts to trim properly. They are these: 1. The character of trimming expresses the use for which the hat is intended.

2. The province of trimming is to decorate the hat and render it becoming to the wearer. 3. The trimming expresses the individual ideas of the trimmer.

When the student can grasp an idea and express it in trimming, so that the effect is pleasing and becoming to the wearer, and the hat appropriate to the use for which it is intended, she has become a trimmer.

When she becomes proficient and can strike out independently, producing new forms of expression for her ideas, she becomes a designer, providing her original ways of doing things result in harmonious millinery.

The Management of Color.

Nothing is more important to the trimmer than the management of color. There are a few rules which the amateur trimmer may safely follow in this matter.

Strong colors and brilliant contrasts are desirable on street hats. By strong colors are meant colors in medium or dark shades or those in lighter tones that will not fade. Ribbons in stripes and plaids provide suitable color contrasts for street hats.

For dress hats the choice of color is not limited.

For the. semi-dress or trimmed hat the most delicate colors should be rejected. Those that will stand considerable exposure to light, will give greatest satisfaction.

Terms Used in Describing Colors.

The terms "shade," "tone" and "tint" are used in describing colors. A color ranges through a number of "shades" to.the darkest and through a number of "tints" to thf lightest "tone." That is, taking a medium tone of anj color, it approaches black through its "shades" and white through its "tints."

There is one important fact that the student may profit by.

When the trimmings selected are shades or tints of the color in the body of the hat, Oe when they are in colors *which have been combined to produce the color in the body of tht hat,* then the effect is harmonious and pleasing. For in stance, a hat in an amethyst shade may be trimmed with red and blue in the shades or tones that combined will produce amethyst.

In selecting colors for trimming the student will be safe in choosing a range that will show a transition from one color to another. The evening sky displays most exquisite color effects where nature shows us rose color melting into blue, or gold changing into green, and innumerable other exquisite color combinations and gradations.

Lines of Grace.

One of the most difficult of the problems that face the trimmer, is that of placing the trimmings Eo that the hat will be graceful on the head and becoming to the wearer. This is the task which makes it necessary lor the trimmer to study her patron. The style of hairdressing (and often the lack of style in hair dressing) have to be reckoned with. The time-honored rule of the milliner is this: "The wearer must look better with her hat on than without it."

When a shape has severe lines, the effort of the trimmer is turned toward softening or breaking them. When trimmings are so placed that they preserve or produce good becoming lines then the trimmer has succeeded in conforming her materials to lines of grace.

Summing up the whole matter of trimming, the essential things to keep in mind are that the character of the trimming must indicate the purpose for which the hat is intended and the best points in the face and coiffure of the wearer of a hat are to be emphasized by its trimming and the bad points concealed or softened.

LESSON XXIII.

Flexible Hats Made by Patterns.

Flexible hats are made of velvet, beaver, silk, cloth or felt. They are made without wire, or with one or two small wires about the brimedge or headsize. In hats of soft braid, small shirring wires are run in the braid, concealed by fibers.

A Flexible Hat of Velvet.

A diagram for one of the most successful patterns for a flexible hat is shown here. It consists of five pieces, four of them alike conical in shape from which the crown is made, and a long slightly curved piece from which the brim is made.

A pattern is to be drafted1 from the diagram given here and cut from manila paper. Jt will consist of two pieces, the brim and a section of the'crown. Use the diagram as a guide, and cut a pattern having the following dimensions:

Crown piece: Height 8 inches; width at the base *iy2* inches; width at middle 7 inches. Brim: Length (outside 'edge,) 36 inches; length inside 23 inches;

width at center 6% inches;.width at ends 5!4 inches.

To Make the Hat of Velvet.

Having cut the pattern, lay it on a strip of velvet li. yards long. When cutting the conical pieces see that the nap runs in one drection in all of them the remaining velvet will provide for the brim.

Having cut the velvet pieces, baste them to an interlining of cape net and cut the interlining by them, allowing the materials to remain basted together.

Sew two crown pieces together on the machine, in a narrow seam, placing the edges, designated by "a-b" in the diagram, together. Next sew the two remaining crown pieces in the same way.

Having made the two halves of the crown, join them in a narrow seam (i inch wide) and complete the crown. Be careful not to stretch the material in sewing, and, if necessary, first baste the pieces together.

For the brim it will be necessary to cut a lining of satin, either white or of the color of the velvet.

To Cut the Lining.

A half yard of satin is sufficient, but requires piecing in one place at the center. Pin the velvet brim and interlining to satin and cut one-half the lining and from this the second half. Join these halves in a narrow seam, and press the seam flat. The satin lining is now to be basted over the interlining.

Trim the lining and interlining one-half inch from the edge of the velvet. Turn the velvet over the lining and blind-stitch the velvet edge to the lining.

Join the ends of the brim piece slipping one end in the other. Turn in the raw edges and slip-stitch the pieces together. Finish the bottom of the crown by turning in the raw edges and overcasting the edges together sew the brim to the crown, and when adjusted, slip-stitch to its edge a heavy satin-covered wire matching the satin lining in color. This wire may be omitted.

Flexible hats are made in other shapes and are known as "collapsible" or "suitcase" hats also. The method of making the various shapes is the same as that just described.

LESSON XXIV.

A Lesson on Laces.

Nearly all the laces used in millinery at present are machine made, but all are known by the name of hand-made or "real" laces from which they are copied. Modern methods in manufacture combine so many different kinds of lace in striving for new effects, that it is often hard to identify a pattern. But milliners must be somewhat familiar witth machine-made laces and are supposed to be able to identify real laces in order to estimate values as well as to classify these fabrics. Some hand-made laces grow more valuable as time passes because they are no longer made and if asked to put a price on any good hand-made lace, the milliner may be fairly certain that the lace has advanced rather than retrogaded in value since its purchase. The student will bear in mind that close imitations of real lace, made by machinery, bear the names of the real laces and are designated as "imitation" when bought and sold.

The most popular laces for millinery use are Chantilly, Mechlin, Alencon, Valenciennes, Irish crichet, Point d'Esprit, French edgings, Duchess and the net top laces. Laces are imported from France, England, Switzerland, Germany and Belgium.

German and Swiss laces are made in lengths of about 4i/£ metres and milliners, new to business have been known to consider these lengths as "remnants" until better informed. French and English laces are woven in continuous lengths and hence are bought in bolts of many yard.

Laces range through a half dozen or more shades, begginning with pure white and passing through ivory, cream color, butter color and ecru to deep ecru. Very few pure white laces are used. Cream colored lace is usually meant when white is designated. Light butter color is sold as cream color.

According to the manner of weaving and finishing the ed.i ges, laces are classified as "insertions," "edgings," "galoons,'! "barb" and "all-overs." An edging is finished with scallops or points along one edge and is straight along the other. An insertion is straight on both edges. A galoon is scalloped or irregular on both edges and is meant to be applied-to other fabrics, while a barb or scarfing lace is wide and finished alike, or nearly alike, on both edges. "All-over" lace shows the same pattern all over the ground.

In ordering laces these names should be used to distinguish the varieties.

To Identify Laces.

It is in this matter of identification that the milliner will find the greatest difficulty. But it is not necessary to go into all the intricate details of the' manufacture of the old hand-made laces from which the others take their names. Usually the form of the mesh is relied Upon to classify a pattern. In "real" laces the mesh is uneven, the openings varying somewhat, while the precision of machinery is observable in manufactured lace and the mesh is uniform, with unvarying regularity of stitch. One determines easily, whether lace is made by hand or machinery, by practice in observing the mesh. To distinguish between "needle-point" and "bobbin" lace, examine the threads and find whether they are tied like a button-hole stitch or are distinctly looped, or whether they are simply plaited or interwoven. If tied or looped the mesh is "needle-point" and if plaited or interwoven the mesh is "bobbin" lace. These two kinds are sometimes combined, as when a needle-point motif is applied to a bobbin-made net. Besides needle-point and bobbin and pillow laces, there are crocheted laces. Figure 1 shows the timplest form of net (much magnified.) Figure 2 shows a Brussels ground and figure 3 Alencon.

Figures, 4, 5, 6 show filling stitches. In figure 7 "brides" or "ties" are pictured, and in figure 8 "picots," used especially for outer edges, are shown. A great variety of stitches is possible, and the ingenuity of lace makers has resulted in the many different nets as shown in figure9. A con fusing number of names, results from the attempt to distinguish new designs (which become popular) from types of lacee from which they are adapted; but it is only the specialist who needs to try to keep up with them. The student hould learn to distinguish between hand-made and machine-made laces, between needle-point, and bobbin laces, and tell when a pattern is a combination of both.

She should recognize the laces most in use at a glance, and a little observation will make her familiar with the'

Study examples, of Brussels, Mechlin, Cluny, Chantilly, Point d'Alencon, Argentan, Point d'Esprit, Valenciennes, Duchess and Point de Venise laces. These, with Irish crochet, Applique, Guipure, Honiton, Escurial and the net top laces will make it possible for the student to learn the characteristics of all the well known types. The study of lace is an intricate one, and the following classification will help to simplify it.

French laces include:

Valenciennes, Escurial, Alencon, Chantilly Duchesse Argentan, Point d'Esprit, Renaissance, French edgings.

Flemish laces include:

German and Swiss laces include:

Brussels and Mechlin laces.

Point Anglaise, Honiton, Guipure, Point deLierre, Torchon.

Irish laces include:

Point de Venise, Rose Point, Oriental, Batiste, and net top laces.

Irish Crochet, Irish Point, Baby Iriib,

As the greater part of laces used in millinery are machinemade, they are modifications of hand-made laces, which they strive to copy. One cannot make lace by any mechanism which will be just like lace made by hand because any machine however wonderful, has limitations as compared with the hand and brain of the lace maker, working together. Therefore designers of laces, to be made by machinery are

Fig. 10 Nets of Various Patterns.

adapting their designs to mechanical workmanship and getting away from the designs of bygone hand-workers more or less. It is this which makes it difficult to identify some machine-made laces according to classifications pf hand-made laces.

CPSIA information can be obtained
at www.ICGtesting.com
Printed in the USA
BVOW07s1333021017
496475BV00011B/274/P

The Trial at Large of Samuel Wild Mitchell, a Weaver in Spitalfields, for The Wilful Murder of his Own Daughter, a Child Nine Years of Age, by Cutting her Throat with a Razor

Anonymous

The Making of Modern Law collection of legal archives constitutes a genuine revolution in historical legal research because it opens up a wealth of rare and previously inaccessible sources in legal, constitutional, administrative, political, cultural, intellectual, and social history. This unique collection consists of three extensive archives that provide insight into more than 300 years of American and British history. These collections include:

Legal Treatises, 1800-1926: over 20,000 legal treatises provide a comprehensive collection in legal history, business and economics, politics and government.

Trials, 1600-1926: nearly 10,000 titles reveal the drama of famous, infamous, and obscure courtroom cases in America and the British Empire across three centuries.

Primary Sources, 1620-1926: includes reports, statutes and regulations in American history, including early state codes, municipal ordinances, constitutional conventions and compilations, and law dictionaries.

These archives provide a unique research tool for tracking the development of our modern legal system and how it has affected our culture, government, business – nearly every aspect of our everyday life. For the first time, these high-quality digital scans of original works are available via print-on-demand, making them readily accessible to libraries, students, independent scholars, and readers of all ages.

The BiblioLife Network

This project was made possible in part by the BiblioLife Network (BLN), a project aimed at addressing some of the huge challenges facing book preservationists around the world. The BLN includes libraries, library networks, archives, subject matter experts, online communities and library service providers. We believe every book ever published should be available as a high-quality print reproduction; printed on-demand anywhere in the world. This insures the ongoing accessibility of the content and helps generate sustainable revenue for the libraries and organizations that work to preserve these important materials.

The following book is in the "public domain" and represents an authentic reproduction of the text as printed by the original publisher. While we have attempted to accurately maintain the integrity of the original work, there are sometimes problems with the original work or the micro-film from which the books were digitized. This can result in minor errors in reproduction. Possible imperfections include missing and blurred pages, poor pictures, markings and other reproduction issues beyond our control. Because this work is culturally important, we have made it available as part of our commitment to protecting, preserving, and promoting the world's literature.

GUIDE TO FOLD-OUTS MAPS and OVERSIZED IMAGES

The book you are reading was digitized from microfilm captured over the past thirty to forty years. Years after the creation of the original microfilm, the book was converted to digital files and made available in an online database.

In an online database, page images do not need to conform to the size restrictions found in a printed book. When converting these images back into a printed bound book, the page sizes are standardized in ways that maintain the detail of the original. For large images, such as fold-out maps, the original page image is split into two or more pages

Guidelines used to determine how to split the page image follows:

• Some images are split vertically; large images require vertical and horizontal splits.
• For horizontal splits, the content is split left to right.
• For vertical splits, the content is split from top to bottom.
• For both vertical and horizontal splits, the image is processed from top left to bottom right.

THE

TRIAL

AT LARGE

OF

SAMUEL WILD MITCHELL,

A WEAVER IN SPITALFIELDS,

FOR THE

𝕮𝖎𝖑𝖋𝖚𝖑 𝕸𝖚𝖗𝖉𝖊𝖗

OF

HIS OWN DAUGHTER,

A CHILD NINE YEARS OF AGE,

BY

CUTTING HER THROAT WITH A RAZOR.

Which was tried at the Sessions-House in the Old Bailey, before SIR ARCHIBALD MACDONALD, Knt. Lord Chief Baron of His Majesty's Court of Exchequer, January 12, 1805.

INCLUDING

His Confession before the Magistrate,

HIS DEFENCE, &c. &c.

TAKEN IN SHORT-HAND.

LONDON

PUBLISHED BY JOHN FAIRBURN, 146, MINORIES.

[*Price Sixpence*]

TRIAL, &c.

Samuel Mitchell, alias Samuel Wild Mitchell, was indicted for that he, on the 18th of December, 1804, not having the fear of God before his eyes, but being moved and seduced by the instigation of the Devil, wilfully, maliciously, and with malice aforethought, did mortally wound Sarah Mitchell, by striking, cutting, and penetrating her throat with a razor, made of iron and steel, and inflicting with it a wound of four inches in length, and two inches in depth, of which mortal wound she instantly died, and so the Jurors say, that he, the said Samuel Mitchell, the aforesaid Sarah Mitchell did kill and murder against the statute, and against the King's peace.

The Case was opened by Mr. Knapp as follows

GENTLEMEN, I have to lay before you the outlines of the painful facts against the prisoner at the bar, namely, for the wilful murder of his own child

Gentlemen, I am not calling your attention either with respect to the nature of the crime, or with respect to the prisoner at the bar, so as to prejudice your minds either with the guilt or the innocence of the prisoner. I shall confine myself to a brief narrative of facts *only*, which I have to lay before you, abstaining from making
any

any observations from the nature of the evidence which I am afraid you will say I am well warranted to make. It is your duty to decide upon the facts, whether the prisoner is guilty or is not of the full charge.

Gentlemen, The prisoner was a weaver lodging in Wheeler street, Spitalfields, which is in the parish of Christ-church, in the county of Middlesex, he was a married man and previous to the time of this transaction, there had been many words between him and his wife, and the very day before this unfortunate transaction took place there had a separation taken place between him and his wife, and on the preceding night the daughter of the prisoner at the bar had gone to the lodgings which her mother had occupied, and had taken the day before.

On the next morning she returned and was employed in quilling, which is putting silk on a shuttle for her father to weave with, she went up to her father's room about twelve at noon, a little before that the prisoner called out to Mrs Nicholls, who lived in the two pair of stairs room, under the room in which the prisoner lived, and asked what it was o'clock, he was answered by the witness, it was about half after eleven; and between that and half past twelve the offence which is imputed to the prisoner at the bar will be satisfactorily proved to you, in the course of that hour the deed was committed, for very soon after twelve o'clock the prisoner went out of the house, and a person of the name of Godby came in, and went up into the room, and when he came there he saw a miserable spectacle, the daughter of the

the prisoner laying on the floor with her throat cut from one ear to the other and therefore there is a probability of this fact, that he was the only person who could have done the deed. but, unfortunately for the prisoner, we do not rest upon any probability, or any supposition

Gentlemen, after the prisoner had done this deed, he went out of the house, he goes to a person he had known many years, a Mr. Dellfour, he invites him to come with him for the purpose of conversation; he goes with him to the Cock and Magpie in Worship street, and when there the prisoner desires to have some conversation— he said that he had something to communicate very important Dellfour had evidenced in his mind he had something important to impart to him, and seeing there were strangers in the room, told him he had better not communicate any thing before strangers They staid in this public house some time, they drank a pot of beer together, and then went out.

The conversation was this —Ned, I shall die; upon which Dellfour immediately supposed there was some degree of illness about him He asked him what was the matter, he had no idea to what that could particularly apply. What do you mean by that said Dellfour —Upon which Mitchell said, " I have killed my Sally, and I shall die for it " Dellfour asked him what he meant to do; Mitchell told him he wanted to go down to Shadwell, he had two friends there that were concerned in the rope-manufactory, and said, they will let me have a shilling or two to help me, that I may live while I am in goal.

B

Gen-

Gentlemen, there is a compleat confession of the prisoner, that he had killed his daughter --In the course of the day he wandered about the streets till the evening, and then he finds his way to his son-in-law's house, and there he is apprehended he there acknowledges to the officer that he did the fact. The officers went to his room—I will not repeat again the situation of the deceased, but a razor was found there, open, and covered with blood within four or five feet of the unfortunate deceased, and at the time the child was found, the blood was actually warm After this had taken place, and the Coroner had done what his duty required him to do, the prisoner was taken before a magistrate, and after every merciful warning from the magistrate, he voluntarily chose to depose, and did confess the whole of this horrid transaction

Gentlemen, these are the whole circumstances of the case, if you can form a rational doubt of the truth of what I have been stating to you, give him the benefit of that doubt, but if the circumstances are so, that they must compel any rational mind to say, the prisoner at the bar is guilty, it is your bounden duty, though it is a painful task for you to perform, to deliver over to justice the person of the prisoner at the bar, who has so offended the laws of God and his country, that he may suffer for so horrible a crime as that with which he is charged.

WITNESSES

WITNESSES FOR THE PROSECUTION.

Examined by Mr. Knapp.

JAMES GODBY deposed, that he had been married to the daughter of the prisoner for more than eight years, that the prisoner lived on the 18th of December last in Wheeler street, almost opposite Flower-de-luce court, Spitalfields, in the parish of Christ-church, that the prisoner was a married man, that he lodged in the top room of the house, his wife and his child Sally, the deceased had lived with him, but he and his wife had been seperated the day before this horrid transaction. The prisoner at the bar was a weaver, and Sally, the deceased, used to be employed in winding quills for her father He saw the prisoner at nine o'clock in the morning of this transaction, and did not see him again on that day, till about ten o'clock at night, he saw the prisoner at the house where he, the witness, lodged, and he told him he should not come into his room. About half past twelve on the same day, after he had been to the warehouse with his work, he went up to see him, and when he came into his room he saw the deceased lying in her blood, but did not take notice of the wound, he was so alarmed, he went down to the room under the prisoner's, and told Mrs Nichols, who lived in that room, he then went away· He had some of his master's property

about

about him, and that he carried home ; he returned a second time, and went into the room again, and saw Mr Kennedy the officer there.

MRS NICHOLS deposed, that she lived in the room immediately under the prisoner, that she was at home on the 18th of December, and said that the prisoner's wife had been with him that morning, that she had a light of her (to light his fire) before eleven o'clock, and that she heard Sally, the deceased, go up stairs, on her return from Spitalfields charity school, about twelve o'clock, she knew it was the little girl by the step, and that when she got in her father's room, she heard the quil-wheel go, and she heard the prisoner's loom make a noise, which it usually did when he was weaving, shortly after she heard a woman go down stairs, and after that she heard a man's foot, but did not then see either of them : That the prisoner had previously called out to her, a little before twelve, to know what o'clock it was, and that Godby, the former witness, came to her in about half an hour after she heard the quil-wheel go and the noise of the prisoner's loom when he was weaving, that she went up with him, and saw Sally, the deceased, lying in her gore of blood, that she saw nothing of the wound, was afraid of going into the room, and called out to the Landlord, "Murder !" upon which he came up.

WM. BYRON deposed, that he was on the 18th of December the Landlord of the house, No 24, Wheeler street, but had since removed, and that the prisoner at that time lodged in the garrat.—That on the alarm of murder, he went up stairs, and

and lifted the deceased up by the waist, in doing which her head fell back, and the gash appeared to him, he then gave the alarm, that her throat was cut, and desired them to go for a surgeon, and for her father, who he supposed was at the Elder-tree public house just by he then looked round the room to see if he could find any instrument, but could not He then observed the quill-wheel was bloody, and the track of blood about room, her cap was bloody, lying in the room, and she was all over blood, and so was he

EDWARD DELIFOUR, a journeyman broad silk weaver, saw the prisoner on the 18th, between the hours of twelve and one, at his apartments, No. 26, Skinner-street, Shoreditch He was at work, and the prisoner knocked at his door, upon which he let him in. The prisoner asked him to go down stairs with him, as he had something particular to communicate. He refused to leave his work unless he would tell him his business; the prisoner then said something had happened that day which never had happened before, and that he should go to Newgate Seeing him in that violent perturbation of mind, he reluctantly left his work, (the prisoner had gone down stairs,) anxious to know the cause of it, he went down stairs and found him at the street door; they went about 50 yards from the witness's door, the prisoner then, with a countenance full of grief, turned round to him and said, "Ned, I shall die!" The witness asked him what had happened, or what was the matter with him, the prisoner said directly to him, "I have killed my Sally." the witness asked him if the child was dead, the prisoner

soner said, " Yes, I have cut her head half off "It
was a very severe morning, and the prisoner was
shivering with cold—the prisoner desired the witness to go with him into a public house, that he
might warm himself and have something to drink;
they went into the first public house they came to,
which was the Cock and Magpie, in Worship-
street, and had a pot of beer—the prisoner called
for it, and a pipe of tobacco There were three
men and a woman there, intire strangers to the
witness—the prisoner then said to the witness in
the tap-room, " Sit down, I have something to
say to you ' Seeing them strangers in the room,
the witness thought it imprudent to speak before
them, desiring the prisoner at the time, if he had
any thing to say to him, not to say it there, in
about a quarter of an hour they went out. The
witness asked the prisoner where he was going,
and what he meant to do with himself—he said he
was going to Shadwell to see two friends of his
who were rope-makers, who would, when he was
in prison, allow him a shilling or two, he then
asked when the Sessions would begin—the witness
told him, he said he would give himself up to
justice and suffer, with this remark, it would
make no odds to him if they cut him in a thou-
sand pieces, for that when he went hundreds
would go at the same minute The witness told
him he should not have killed his child The prisoner looked him in the face and said, " I know
that—do not you retort on me now it is done."
The witness accompanied him as far nearly as
Whitechapel-church, then shook him by the hand,
and saw him no more till he saw him at the office;
the witness said the Magistrate sent for him, and he
gave

gave the same account at that time as he now gave. When in the public house with him, he observed a small quantity of blood on one of his hands.

THOMAS GRICE, a watchman of Bethnal-green, said, that two men came to their watch-house and gave information that the prisoner was in Hare-street, at his daughter's, and there the witness apprehended him and took him to Bethnal-green watch-house, and then went and delivered him up to the Officer of Spitalfields watch-house, as soon as he saw the prisoner, the prisoner said he was the man that was guilty of the murder, and resigned himself up

JAMES KENNEDY, an Officer of Worship-street, received information of the murder about one o'clock in the afternoon, and went with Bishop into the prisoner's room, and there saw the deceased laying with her head towards the door, with no cap on, and her throat cut across through the wind-pipe, she had done bleeding when the witness saw her, but the blood lying on the floor was warm. On the block of the quill-wheel there was a quantity of blood, and a track of blood from the wheel to where the body laid. Near the quill-wheel there was a low stool, and at the side of it he found a razor open. It was covered with fresh blood at that time. [This he produced in Court, and a cap of the deceased's, stained with blood, that had fallen from her head.] He, seeing there was no prospect of restoring life, with the assistance of Bishop, put the people out of the room. About twelve at night they received information that he was in Spitalfields watch-house. Armstrong and he went there to satisfy them-

themselves, and saw the prisoner sitting by the watch-house fire. He turned his head round and saw the witness. He said, " Kennedy, I have given you much trouble to-day in searching after me." Armstrong said to him, "What do you mean by that? is your name Mitchell?" he said it was. Armstrong again asked him, did he know he was charged with murdering his own daughter, and said he had seen a cap and a razor found in his room. The prisoner then answered, with that razor he had often shaved himself, and with that razor he committed the horrid deed.

JOSEPH MOSER, Esq. stated, that he was a Magistrate of Worship-street Office, that the prisoner was brought before him to be examined on Wednesday the 19th of December, he took down the whole confession of the prisoner in writing, telling him the consequences in every point of view, and the use that would be made of it after he had signed it, he repeated it over to him several times, he said it was true what he had signed, and he signed it in the Magistrate's presence.

THE
CONFESSION
OF

Samuel Wild Mitchell,

A WEAVER,

FOR THE

WILFUL MURDER

Of his Child, SARAH MITCHELL, aged Nine Years

Taken by JOSEPH MOSER, Esq. Dec 19, 1804

―――――――

I, *Samuel Wild Mitchell*, weaver, late of the parish of Christ Church, Middlesex, now standing at the bar of the Public Office, Worship-street, being fully apprized of the nature of my situation by the Magistrate, and through him made perfectly sensible of the nature of this acknowledgement, do make this free and un-biassed confession, which is taken by own desire:—that I had a daughter named Sally, and my wife had a daughter named Elizabeth, who at one time did live with me, but whom I after-wards took to my apartment, where I instructed her in the art of weaving, and we lived all to-gether, this said daughter of my wife's caused some uneasiness, as I thought, and I thought my wife was more indulgent to her faults, and fa-voured her more than she ought, which was the

C   reason

reason of our separation on the 17th of December last, my wife also took with her Sarah Mitchell whom I loved with the most ardent affection, which vexed me a great deal as I saw there would be a continual dispute, I could not bear the little girl coming to see me, as coming on a visit. I resolved that neither my wife nor me should possess her. I seized the moment of the mother going away, the child was sitting by the fire winding quills, I took the razor from the drawer, my affection made me almost lay it down again, but my resolution overcame that. I turned round and cut her throat. I was too resolute to make a faint attempt, the child was dead in a moment, she neither made noise nor resistance, when I had done the deed the child fell, as I went out I saw her blood, then I ran down stairs. After this act was done to my child Sarah Mitchell, I went to a man named Bell, where I had lived, and left word for him to run and secure my master's work, then I went to Mr Dellfour, and my friends at Wapping. This acknowledgment is free, and made by my own desire.

 Signed   SAMUEL WILD MITCHELL

Dec. 19, 1804   JOSEPH MOSER

  Here ended the proofs for the prosecution, and the Prisoner was called on by the Court for any thing he had to say in his defence, when the wretched man addressed himself to the Court and Jury nearly in the following words —

        PRISONER'

PRISONER's DEFENCE.

My Lord, and Gentlemen of the Jury,

I stand in this place to day an awful spectacle of guilt and disgrace, but I will endeavour to be as collected in my reason as possible though at certain times and seasons I am particularly under heavy pressure of mind, which my wife well knows, and was well aware of it, that I have committed the horrid deed laid to my charge I have no wish to deny, any more than I have to avoid the dreadful punishment that awaits my guilt, to that I am resigned, nor was it my wish from the unfortunate moment of my crime to evade justice, but that I committed the deed maliciously against my poor child, who was the victim of my fatal passion, I solemnly deny. Malice I had none, I declare in the presence of God before whom I stand and make this declaration, and before whose awful tribunal I must shortly appear, instead of bearing to her malice I loved her most tenderly. I had kind love to the child, and wished her not to be from me, and to that love, strange and perverse as it may seem, is owing chiefly the sad cause that brings me here this day I am married to a second wife, by whom this child was my only daughter, we had long known each other before our marriage, when I was in better days, and when she and I were the wife and husband of others I thought I could be happy with her, but I found her temper incompatible with my happiness or her own I found the friends and the family

C 2   with

with which she was connected thought her mar
riage to me degrading to her. Disputes and
controversy, for ten years frequently took place
between us, in which, unhappily, both were in
fault, too much so, those disputes were often
carried to a pitch of fury (and may this sad
spectacle that I now stand be a warning to others
that if they meet with double families to have
more love to their duty), and what tended still
more to exasperate me and aggrevate our dis-
sentions was, that those she called her friends
always sided with her in every thing, whether right or wrong, and many of them, I
am sorry to say, were strenuous professors of
religious principles, were always more ready to
lend a hand to the fomenting of mischief than to
the promotion of charity and peace, may the
Lord forgive them, and take me to himself. Our
disputes at last ended in a mutual agreement to
separate, and the child I so tenderly loved was to go
with her mother, this my unhappy temper and
feeling could not bear, which led me to the fatal
resolution that neither she nor I should have the
child by committing the horrid deed, by putting
an end to her life in the manner I have done! I
pray God Almighty to forgive me, and to direct
you in your decision upon me this day, and
though here I stand an object of sin and misery
yet I hope my unhappy fate will prove an awful
example to those who form second marriages
with children on both sides, against giving way
to intemperate disputes, that may lead them, as
they have done me, to acts of desperation and
vengeance, beyond the control of reason or re-
flection. If my wife was present she could vouch
an

and prove that it was impossible I could ever have deliberately executed such an act. She could testify that my disposition was not cruel, and that when I have been the most resolute to good purposes, unfortunately, under agitations of mind, or provocations of temper, such has been my weakness. I am not always the same man; and, under such circumstances, I have very frequently been led into excesses of frenzy, which, in cool moments, have astonished me. Once in particular, forced by distress (when I had no work) to apply for relief at my parish workhouse, I had come too late in the day, when, wound up by disappointment to madness, I broke as many windows as cost the parish four pounds for the repair, and yet the parish-officers though they might have punished me, did not, knowing that my act was the result of a mind deranged —May the Lord forgive me, and take me to himself! I must die a spectacle of sin and horror!—There is one single point I have to say, which my wife could attest, if she was here, as she was well acquainted with my misery, as well as my mother's who would frequently go into the same way. she was a very sensible woman, she would frequently ask me to cut her hair, for, unless her hair was kept cut in a very particular close manner, her weakness was upon her. So it has been with me.

––––––––––

The *Lord Chief Baron* informed the Jury that the fact of a person's being overcome by any sudden paroxysm of passion to commit a deed

of

of so flagitious a nature, operated as no justification of the crime. If God afflicted any man with a temporary, or occasional want of reason, that was a different question. There, from the mere occasional suspension of the reasoning faculties, the crime might have been committed but such could by no means be compared to the case where the dereliction of the reasoning faculties had been occasioned either by the contemplation of a circumstance by which alone the mind was affected, or by which, after its completion, the mind could be supposed capable of being agitated. Here a strange mixture of affection was discernible amidst the cruelty which had prompted the perpetration of the deed, but he could see nothing in the case to induce him to point out to the Jury any distinction between this case and the various other cases of a similar kind which presented themselves

The Jury immediately found the prisoner—
GUILTY.

His appearance at the time of his defence, was squalid and wretched in the extreme, his hair was grey, and his head was covered with an old miserable night-cap.

The prisoner was then informed that he stood convicted of the wilful murder of *Sarah Mitchell,* and was asked by *Mr. Shelton* the Clerk of the Court what he had to say for himself, that the Court should not give him judgment to die, according to law?

The prisoner made no reply.

Mr.

Mr. *Recorder*, in a style the most solemn, awful, and impressive, then addressed the wretched man as follows

Prisoner at the bar, you have been convicted by the verdict of a most attentive and merciful Jury, of the most horrid crime of Murder! Odious as this offence is in the eyes of God and man, your case presents itself with every possible feature of aggravation, the object of your blood-thirsty vengeance was on an infant whose first efforts of speech hailed you by the endearing name of *father*, who nature directed Let to look up for affection she has found more than savage cruelty, and where she turned to her guardian and protector she has found her destroyer and murderer! The voice of God has declared that "he who sheddeth man's blood, by man shall his blood be shed." A very short time remains for you to supplicate the throne of Grace for that mercy, which public justice and security affordeth you to expect in this world, I sincerely hope, that, from the interval which has passed between the commission of your horrid crime and the present moment, you have been employed in imploring pardon of the Almighty, and it is my most fervent wish, that your prayer may, through the mercy of the Redeemer find acceptance —Thus having discharged my duty, it only remains for me to pass upon you the dreadful sentence of the law, which is, That you, *Samuel Hird Mitchell*, be taken from hence to the place from whence you came, and from thence you be taken to a place of execution on Monday next, and there be hanged by your neck till you be dead, and that your body

be

be after disected and anatomised, pursuant to the statute that is made in such cases and provided

The Court was crowded in every part, and particularly with women, and not only those, but the Jury, the Counsel, and nearly all present, were melted into tears.

FINIS.

Printed by J H HART, 23, Warwick-Square

CPSIA information can be obtained
at www.ICGtesting.com
Printed in the USA
BVOW07s1333021017

496475BV00011B/275/P